PROFITABLE
PRACTICE

PROFITABLE
PRACTICE

WHY A VETERINARY PRACTICE
IS AN EXCEPTIONAL INVESTMENT

TIMOTHY A. BROWN & JACKIE JOACHIM

Copyright © Timothy Brown and Jackie Joachim, 2019

Published by ECW Press
665 Gerrard Street East
Toronto, Ontario M4M 1Y2

Printing: Friesens   5   4   3   2   1

PRINTED AND BOUND IN CANADA

LIBRARY AND ARCHIVES CANADA
CATALOGUING IN PUBLICATION

Title: Profitable practice : why a veterinary practice is an exceptional investment / Timothy A. Brown & Jackie Joachim.
Other titles: Profitable practice (2019)

Names: Brown, Timothy A. (Timothy Adam), author. | Joachim, Jackie, author.

Identifiers: Canadiana 20190054166 | ISBN 9781550229400 (hardcover)

Subjects: LCSH: Veterinary medicine—Practice. | LCSH: Veterinary medicine—Finance.

Classification: LCC SF756.4 .B76 2019 | DDC 636.089068—DC23

Text design: Tania Craan

MIX
Paper from
responsible sources
FSC® C016245

This book is dedicated to Roy Brown,
founder of ROI Corporation.
His vision and pioneering drive has allowed
professionals of many disciplines to retire with
dignity and profitably.

Table of Contents

. . . .

* *

As co-owners of ROI Corporation, Brokerage, Timothy A. Brown and I have made many efforts to help our health care clients with all aspects of their practices. Our company specializes in providing appraisals and practice sales services for health care business owners. In addition, we consult with and provide many related services from financing to locum placements and practice management advice. Many years of service in the health care industry has provided us with a multitude of resource information and expertise for would-be health care practitioners, including veterinarians. We share this knowledge in many ways: in newsletters, private consultations, books and through our magazine *Profitable Practice*.

I encourage you to read this book written by Timothy A. Brown (CEO of ROI Corp.) and Jackie

Joachim (COO of ROI Corp.). I know how hard Timothy and Jackie work to satisfy our clients' service requirements and provide them with the most current and valuable information available.

High school students contemplating a career in veterinary medicine will find it a very useful resource—as will veterinary students at every level in their university studies. Finally, practicing veterinarians at every stage of their careers will take away valuable insights that will ensure their continued success as practitioners.

Happy reading and may you all have long and profitable careers.

SANDY EVANS

INTRODUCTION

. . . .

"This one pivotal development spearheaded by my father allowed for the sale of countless thousands of health care practices to this day."
— Timothy A. Brown

Today, health care practices (dental, veterinarian, optometry, etc.) have substantial value and are sold daily nationwide. That was not always the case. Roy Brown, our founder, began selling dental supplies in 1948, at the age of 18. He joined the Associated Dentists Cooperative (ADC) as a junior salesman and was assigned a territory based out of London, Ontario.

During Roy Brown's 26-year career with the ADC, he introduced many services relevant to the profession. Roy became ADC's general manager and later president. Noticing that many of the board member practitioners were aging and their retirement was nearing, he wondered, *Who would take over their established practices?*

Roy wanted to assist dentists and other health care professional practice owners to leave their businesses with dignity and profitably, and so he formed ROI Management (later renamed ROI Corporation, Brokerage) in 1974.

At first, health care professionals were skeptical. When most health care professionals retired, they simply packed their bags and locked their office doors. Few saw any value in their practice's patient list, their equipment or their practice's "goodwill."

In 1974, Roy met with a very successful dentist who was frustrated at the prospect of shutting down his very well-equipped and successful practice. He commissioned Roy to act as his agent and to find him a replacement dentist to take over. He set his asking price at $28,000.

Later that year, Roy identified a suitable buyer, a contract was negotiated and what appears to be the very first "brokered" sale of a dental practice was documented in Canada. The price paid? Exactly $28,000!

This one pivotal development, spearheaded by Roy Brown, allowed for the sale of countless thousands of health care practices to this day. The result is a full-fledged appraisal and brokerage industry devoted entirely to the buying and selling of professional practices. This industry appraises, educates, promotes and presents all avenues for the health care professional to be successful.

Forty-five years later, the appraisal and sale of professional practices is not only our business but it has been and continues to be our passion! We believe, as Roy did all those years ago, that practice owners deserve to retire with dignity and profitably.

Part I

. . . .

WHY A VETERINARY PRACTICE IS AN EXCEPTIONAL INVESTMENT

CHAPTER 1

Starting Out

• •

Who Are Veterinary Professionals and What Do They Do?
This important question is answered here for those
in high school who are contemplating a veterinary
career as well as for students at every level in university who are choosing what to focus on when they
graduate.

When you decide to become a veterinarian, you
will likely do so because of your love of and interest
in animals. As you proceed through school, embark on
your career and discover your passions, as in all professions, there will be decisions to make: will you work
with small or large animals, exotics, equine or other?
The amount of money you will earn is dependent
on your location, lifestyle, challenges and schedule.
Today's veterinarians are not limited to only small and
large animal practices; in addition to the possibilities

below, you may also find opportunities in wildlife and conservation, government and the pet food industry.

The wonderful thing about choice is that you can always change your mind, and you certainly do not need to lock into one or the other for a lifetime. There are many practices, for example, that see both small and large animals.

So as a future business owner, the first question to ask is: what kind of animals do you want to treat?

Small Animal Veterinarians

A veterinarian in a small animal practice mainly works defined hours with small household pets such as cats, dogs, rabbits, gerbils, hamsters, and birds. They may also decide to include exotics in the practice— ferrets, guinea pigs, snakes and lizards. They usually work in a clinic or hospital environment with one or more veterinarians, and they are responsible for care that includes daily client appointments, vaccinations, check-ups, surgery (such as spays, neuters and other more complicated procedures), providing advice to owners, dispensing prescription pharmaceuticals as well as performing euthanasia. In cities and towns that do not have emergency out-of-hours service, the small animal veterinarian usually also takes part in emergency care outside normal business hours.

As a small animal sole practitioner, you must also be prepared to become an entrepreneur. This means that you must hire and manage staff, ensure the bills are paid and select appropriate equipment—all while providing excellent client service.

Large Animal Veterinarians

A veterinarian in a large animal practice works with cattle, sheep, horses, goats, elk, deer and pigs, among others. They usually work from a central clinic, but rather than the animals coming to them, they travel to the client. A large animal practitioner is responsible for preventative care programs, herd health, reproductive management (pregnancy checking), newborn management, surgery, treatment of ill or injured animals, dispensing pharmaceuticals, vaccination, providing advice, euthanasia and so on. These veterinarians usually carry all the equipment and tools needed with them in their vehicles.

> **Tip:** watch the British TV program *All Creatures Great and Small*, based on the books of veterinary surgeon Alf Wight; this late '70s series provides a wonderfully realistic depiction of the life of a country veterinarian.
>
> Some large animal veterinarians work in slaughterhouses where they make sure that the animals and their meat are healthy. It is a well-paying, steady job often with regular hours.

Equine Veterinarian

As an equine practitioner, you may decide to work with horses that are used for pleasure, racing, breeding or performance. An equine practitioner works out of a clinic; like any large animal veterinarian, they usually travel to their clients. They are responsible for preventative care programs, reproductive management (pregnancy checking), lameness diagnosis, surgery, vaccination, providing advice, euthanasia and the like.

Marine Animal Veterinarian
This practitioner is involved with fish, porpoises, whales, etc., in aquariums or research centres. There are limited positions available in this field.

Exotic/Zoo Animal Veterinarian
A veterinarian who works in a zoo environment interacts with a wide variety of species, often exotic, and is responsible for their care and nutrition while these animals live in limited spaces. Again, there are few positions in this field.

Veterinarian for Laboratory Animals for Research
This fast-growing area of business needs veterinarians. These practitioners usually work with mice, rats, fish, rabbits, birds, dogs, cats—any animal that is used for research purposes for both animal and human benefit. This occupation demands a veterinarian also possess a research skillset. This career includes supervising and training employees, students and researchers as well as caring for the animals.

Pharmaceutical Company Veterinarian
These companies need veterinarians to create, test and advise on the drugs that are commonly used on animals. Other skillsets are also required as these veterinarians may be asked to do research as well as attend conferences to gain more knowledge about the products they produce.

The Canadian Veterinary Reserve (CVR)

An interesting option for veterinary volunteer work exists with the CVR. Established in 2006, it has a national membership of qualified Canadian volunteer veterinarians who are available to rapidly assist governments in response to outbreaks of foreign animal diseases and other large-scale emergencies and disasters that affect animals. The CVR membership program is administered and operated by the Canadian Veterinary Medical Association (CVMA). It currently has 474 members with 245 of them having received formal training. A compensation package has been developed so that reservists and their private practices neither suffer financially nor profit excessively while they are being trained or deployed. For more information, visit CanadianVeterinarians.net.

A Note on Veterinary Governing Bodies

No matter where you decide to practice in Canada, or whether you set up a small, large or mixed animal practice, you must be licensed by the veterinary regulatory body in that province; this body may be a medical association or a college of veterinarians.

Early Career

Where to Practice?

Choosing the type of veterinary medicine you want to practice will determine in large part where you locate as an associate and/or as a practice owner. Veterinarians who choose a small animal career often locate in major cities, since the highest density of pet and animal owners are located in urban centres. Practising in an urban centre has many advantages as many new grads want the urban lifestyle with all its cultural benefits and attractions as well as the advantage of having family and friends close by.

However, locating in a major urban centre can have drawbacks. Competition in major centres like Toronto, Calgary and Vancouver can be fierce, and opportunities may become scarce. Our experiences with health care professionals reveal some of the happiest and most successful people are found in smaller towns and rural areas. Here the health care professional is more often than not highly regarded, and they can choose to become a leader and pillar in their community. Competition and the cost of living and practicing are much lower and both the financial and non-financial rewards are generally higher. We strongly urge recent graduates to consider locating in a smaller community, at least for the first few years of their careers.

To Associate or Not

Most graduates will associate for the first five years. By doing so, they will learn to diagnose and treat a variety of species. They will work in a clinic with an older professional or in a well-established practice with multiple veterinarians. In the ideal situation, the older professional will become your mentor and the benefits you receive will be many. If you are alert and open-minded, you will learn daily from your mentor's example and tutelage—not only clinical skills and procedures but also business and practice management lessons. You may learn what not to do, as well as what to do when you are on your own.

Many professionals we have met and worked with say that the best advice they would give to a graduating class is to first become the best clinician you can be; perfect your skills and never stop learning or wanting to know more about what you do. When you have developed these qualities and you have ingested enough practice management skills—especially when it comes to staff and staff policies and client/patient relationships—go out and buy the practice that suits your philosophy and needs the best.

Mentorship: The Benefits

Most established professionals we talk to mention a special someone who helped them develop their skills and approach to veterinary medicine—someone who turned on a light for them and gifted them with crucial career knowledge. The mentor/student relationship is common to all health care professions. It may have been that special instructor in university or the first owner who hired you as an associate for their practice. It may be the result of a continuing education (CE) course you take. Whoever it turns out to be, cherish the relationship and learn your craft under their guidance. The time will come when you might very well be the mentor and pay it forward to the next aspiring young veterinarian. The rewards are many compared to the extra time and effort you will exert in being either a mentor or a student.

CHAPTER 2

The Next Big Career
Move: Ownership

• •

Once you have practiced for a number of years and
you have paid off any student or other kind of debt,
it is time for the big decision. Are you ready to make
the move to ownership? For some, this day may never
come; for others, it can't come soon enough. Before
we get to the essential steps in buying a practice
(should you decide to do so), consider what follows.

Setting Up a New Practice

If you have a true entrepreneurial spirit, starting up
is an option. It is not for the faint of heart though.
You must be prepared to go for a number of months
without making money or being able to take a draw.
You must consider the option of an outside source of
income to cover your personal expenses until your

new practice can generate sufficient profit to pay you. So where do you start?

Location, Location, Location

Every realtor will tell you how important it is to find the best possible place for your new clinic. Consider important things like demographics, new housing developments and current competition. These factors will definitely have an impact on the marketing strategies you choose to pursue and ultimately whether your new practice will survive and thrive.

Size and Layout of the Practice Facility

Typically a small animal practitioner has a small reception area where clients come in with their pets. This area should be clean with a small, comfortable sitting area where the client and patient wait to be moved to an examination room. The number of examination rooms is dictated by the number of clients you have and the number of associates and/or technicians who deliver their services for your practice. If you provide surgery on-site, this requires another area with sterilization facilities and surgical instruments. Many small animal veterinarians provide kennel facilities for overnight patients. This may require some staff to supervise and oversee the operation. Many practices also provide a room for an on-site groomer. A growing number of urban clinics now feature pet "spa" options that pamper as well as treat their patients.

By contrast, large animal veterinarians generally have small practice offices as most of their services are provided off-site where the animals are kept. All clinics require safe and secure places to store equipment and supplies, including drugs and other medications, as well as a waste disposal system. Practitioners who specialize in the treatment of specific animals (e.g., exotics) may need additional instruments, equipment and facilities. A washroom, staff room and your own personal office must be included in the planning of your practice.

Deciding on the size and layout of the office will be a function of many things: number of clients per day, number of associates, animals treated, procedures done, special patient requirements, practice growth and expansion and many more. Take into account that you may wish to expand at some future date. That possibility leads you to another major question.

Do you buy or lease your practice's space? Buying means you'll need additional start-up finances. But when you reach retirement, you will not only sell your practice but the building that practice is in. The major advantage of ownership is its possible financial reward in the increase of property value over time. Also, owning your facility allows for future expansion and a personally designed clinic set-up plan. However, it can also place limitations on your ability to move your practice to another location prior to your retirement. In our experience, a greater number of veterinarians lease their practice space in a location that suits their needs and finances best.

Numbers

Of course, we saved the best for last. The cost of a new practice can start at $350,000 depending on the size, location and how you want to equip the clinic. Money is required for negotiating a lease, plans, building and waiting for an inspection. Be prepared for this phase to last at least six months. The amounts budgeted for growth, expenses and paying back the bank are all-important numbers to be acutely and sometimes painfully aware of. When you are going to a financial institution to ask for this important start-up loan, always be prepared with a business plan. Also, do not forget to ask for a line of credit to help float expenses for at least three to six months. The new practice will take a little bit of time to get off the ground, and the last thing you want is to fail due to lack of capitalization.

Buying a Veterinary Practice

Buying a veterinary practice is a time-consuming, demanding process for any professional; it's a very complex transaction that forces you to make some difficult decisions.

First, as in the case of the start-up, it is important to determine your preferred location for your practice. You may, for example, decide you need to be within a 30-minute drive from home so you are close to family and friends. This limitation has prevented many veterinary professionals from considering thriving practices for sale outside of Canada's major cities but which require relocating. The sooner you commit to an area, the more precise your search can be, so it's best to set your sights on one or two regions.

Other questions that must be answered include:

- How much debt are you prepared to incur—$250,000, $750,000 or more? Many professionals have student loans, car loans, new families, mortgages and other major expenses, and they will need to borrow a large sum of money to buy a practice.
- How many days or hours per week do you want to work? Some practices offer part-time hours that may be more suitable if you have parenting obligations. Others may demand that you work 50–60 hours per week plus some evenings and weekends.
- What is the scope of treatment you can offer, and what must you refer out to another veterinary specialist? Do not overestimate your skills— problems arise when inexperienced practitioners take on cases that they should have referred out.
- What is your preferred clinical working plan and environment?
- What role does hygiene play in your practice and are you comfortable with the existing set-up?
- How fast is your dexterity and operative speed?
- How much full-time experience do you have?
- Will you be expanding your practice to include other services (like animal grooming), associates or specialists in the future? If your long-term goal is to own a large practice, think well ahead. Relocating

is very expensive and has the potential to be a
serious disruption to practice income.

Think about these issues carefully. Once you have
answered these questions, you can begin your search.
Here are 10 key steps in the process.

1. Start by phoning veterinary practice brokers—let
   them know you are in the market and express your
   commitment to thoroughly investigate practices in
   the city, town or area you prefer. Many brokers have
   more buyers than practices for sale.
2. Each practice you consider should have a
   professional appraisal ready for you to review.
   Most brokers ask that you sign a confidentiality
   agreement, which states that your personal
   information and the data supplied to you about the
   owner-practitioner will be protected. This is usually
   done just prior to viewing the appraisal report,
   which should include all operational and financial
   data about the practice. If a proper appraisal is
   not available (complete appraisals are usually
   50–75 pages in length), you are entitled to request
   one. You need that data in order to make an
   informed decision. Also, banks will not lend money
   for a practice purchase without this important
   document.
3. Ask your banker to review the appraisal to
   help determine if you qualify for the funds you
   need. Each bank has a special program to assist
   veterinarians with such purchases.

4. Visit your accountant. This is the most important step to determine your ability to manage the practice. Accountants will also prepare a budget for your personal living expenses and income taxes over and above the office expenses.

5. You're now ready to view a practice. This is usually done after-hours. Most veterinary professionals do not tell their staff the practice is for sale due to the risk of damaging the practice's stability. Staff and clients have been known to leave practices when rumours about a sale circulate because people assume the owner has personal, health or financial problems.

6. Verify the information found in any appraisal or report given to you. For example, counting charts in a practice is something you should do because a chart count will help determine how busy you may be in the future. However, a chart count is a very unreliable way to value the goodwill of a practice. The revenue earned from patients is a far superior indication of value.

7. Brokers usually work exclusively for, and are therefore paid by, the seller; accordingly, their duty under agency law is to represent only the vendor. A broker will provide you with answers to anything you need clarification on and will certainly introduce you to key advisors if you do not currently have one. This allows you to participate with representation, so be sure to include your accountant, lawyer and banker. It is uncommon for two different brokers to be involved in the sale of a veterinary practice.

8. Once you have viewed the practice and performed your own verification of charts, appointment books and financial records, it's time to draft an offer. At this point, it is essential to obtain legal advice. Remember that the Agreement of Purchase and Sale document is designed to be fair to both parties. Since most brokers want your business in the future, they are most likely to treat you fairly. Under agency law, you are entitled to full disclosure of all meaningful business facts about the practice you are purchasing.

9. The agent of the broker will perform most of the negotiations between both veterinary practitioners. They act as the intermediary between the lawyers, accountants and the financial institution, if necessary.

10. Be certain you have investigated the entire process before signing the final offer. If you are not sure, walk away. Do not act too quickly or bow to pressure from anyone who threatens that you may lose this opportunity. There will be other practices for sale in the future. Do not compromise your career because of a rash decision.

CHAPTER 3

Practice Management Issues

· ·

Staffing

Building a staff for your new practice is one of the toughest tasks you will face. Almost every owner when asked "What keeps you up at night?" provides the same answer: staff. The staff you hire, train and mentor are not quite family, not quite friends, not quite equals or peers (at least at first). They have a unique relationship with you that requires you to have special management skills.

You must learn when to be firm with a staff member and ask for better or more effort. You need to know when to back off and give people some space, when to praise, when to seek outside help for a problem and, most important of all, when to let someone go. The best result you can hope for is a staff that works as a team, leaves their egos at the door, is flexible, works well with each other and with your patients and clients. In addition, they should be loyal and professionally committed to do the best job possible. Building this level of staff competency requires a supreme effort on your part. You must become a student of human behaviour and motivation. You should take a number of CE courses delivered by the best minds in the business. Develop a hiring process that screens out candidates, filters through the details and impressions and ultimately selects those who not only fit your expectations but also the expectations of the rest of your staff. To achieve this requires that you be a boss who inspires, motivates and leads.

Successful teams often bond outside of the practice. There may be a common cause or charity that they work for. There may be social and professional events attended by many of the staff after-hours. The key here is that they are optional, limited in number and designed to develop trust and appreciation for each other.

Professionally, many successful teams have regular "huddles" where procedures and expectations are discussed to reach a common and shared understanding and acceptance.

There are times when a staff member may be involved in an illegal activity with regard to your practice—for example, a fraudulent or contractual transgression. Estimates on how many practices are likely to be a victim of some fraudulent activity are high. The worst thing you can do is to be complacent. Regularly checking your reports, bank deposits and supplier payments is crucial. Be particularly careful with regard to the inventory and management of supplies and drugs used in the practice. If any such activity occurs, or you suspect it might be occurring, in your clinic, take action by seeking the advice and intervention of an expert in various fraud schemes. Also manage your own books within the practice and seek outside accounting help to verify your financial affairs. Assuming that your staff would never do any of these things is naive. We have seen many instances of long-time and trusted staff (people who were considered extended family) taking money from a practice. Sadly, this happens more than you might think.

With regard to sexual harassment, once again seek outside legal aid. Whether the harassment involves yourself and/or other members of staff, it can be a very thorny and expensive issue, one that requires the expertise of a lawyer. The best practice is for you and your staff to refrain from any type of "office romance." Additionally, make it clear that offensive comments or actions with regard to race, religion, sexual orientation or gender identity will not be tolerated. Hopefully, you have taken time to develop an employee handbook. Make sure that your staff reads your office manual and that it delineates proper staff procedures and conduct. The manual should include the expected behaviour of your staff with regard to each other as well as with clients and patients. From time to time, the manual should be revised to accommodate legal and contractual conduct changes and any new or improved procedures. It is important that staff have a copy for their own records and initial the copy you retain for yourself.

Many successful teams benefit from a profit sharing program or bonus system based on increased and/ or improved production and service. Staff should be rewarded when your practice is growing and prospering, which results in part from their efforts in providing quality service and attention to your clients' and patients' needs. Profit-sharing plans can be simple or quite complicated and are usually partially based on a percentage of gross income. Again, there are many continuing education courses that detail these arrangements. We always encourage owners to make bonuses and rewards random. It is very common to award these at key times in the year—anniversaries, end of year or Christmas. The unfortunate assumption can be made by staff that these are annual entitlements regardless of whether or not the clinic increases in profitability; it's best to manage expectations through clear communication.

When it comes to hiring, it is common to hire people who are similar to you. After all, you want a harmonious office where everyone gets along. A problem with that strategy is that when we hire people like ourselves, we are usually hiring people with the same strengths and weaknesses as us. Your main focus when building your team should be to find key people who have different skillsets, ones which complement yours. It is critical these people suit your practice. They must be highly skilled professionals who possess the required expertise as well as experientially adept, socially confident and willing to work in your team environment.

The last point we wish to make on this important topic is that people need straightforward direction and this begins with a job description. We all need a clear list of duties and expectations. Communicating the goals and the steps to achieve them are critical. Job descriptions help staff meet your expectations and that results in a team working well together to achieve success.

The Student Becomes Owner, Entrepreneur and Mentor

Once you have assembled the best staff and associates possible, it is time to think as an entrepreneur. *Can I grow my practice? What business plan suits me best—single proprietor, partnership, corporate? Do I have a team I can mentor and count on to carry out my veterinary vision and philosophy?*

Set goals for the short, medium and long term. Short-term goals are those to be achieved within 30 days to a year. Medium are those to be reached in two or three years, and long term goals are in five-year cycles. Surely you have heard by now how important it is to regularly review and alter goals if necessary. Your overall goal is to improve your production and the quality of service you offer. Consider when it may be the right time to bring in a professional consultant to aid in your decision-making or to attend a CE course with this focus.

Midcareer and Beyond

No matter what choices you make with regard to growing your practice or remaining where you are comfortable, your best earning years are ahead of you. Even if you are not overly aggressive in your approach, your practice is likely to grow as your client base does, thanks to the quality and nature of the service your clinic offers. You will likely offer more services, become part of the local business community, make improvements in your staff's performance and develop long-term relationships with many of your clients and their animals. Don't underestimate the value of becoming involved in your community's local projects, fundraisers or business clubs, and remember that there are many rewards to be gained in providing some pro bono work both at home and abroad.

After several years of perfecting your practice and the services you are providing, you are likely, at some point, to want a better work/play division of your time. As the cliché goes, there is a need to step back and smell the roses and enjoy some of the fruits of your labour. This may mean more family time, travel and recreational activities. Millennials seem to have a better grasp of the importance of developing a balance between work and play. This is very much an individual decision that is determined by many factors, but to not give it any thought is to do so at your own peril. There are numerous documented cases of burnout, compassion fatigue and stress-related illness and addiction that cost many practitioners their health and sometimes their livelihood. Be prudent: take some time to leave your work behind and recharge.

CHAPTER 4

The Key to Everything: The Professional Practice Appraisal

. . . .

Many owners think the only time to appraise their practice is when they start thinking about retirement. But, there are many occasions when you should do an appraisal that have nothing to do with retiring or selling. Think about it as taking the temperature of your office. Maybe there is a life-changing event occurring such as a matrimonial event or bringing in a new associate or partner. The list goes on. If you don't think about an appraisal only when it is time to sell, then how do you know when exactly the right time for one is? What is the best course of action? What will you do after retirement? These are just a few of the questions that arise.

Many veterinarians hire an associate with the expectation that they will be the heir apparent. This does not always work out, but many veterinarians wish to take this path of action. Some thought should be given to whether or not you wish to be a part of the transition process. Do you take on a reduced workload for a year or two and partner with the associate until your clients have familiarized themselves with the change in ownership? Or do you walk away and depart with no ties to your former practice?

Over the years, we have advocated for both decisions. It is, after all, a very personal choice. In our experience, many practitioners choose to stay on, help with the transition but soon (around six months or so) reach a point where they are ready to cut ties and move on with the next phase of their lives.

If the thought of selling or retiring does enter your mind, getting an appraisal is important because it gives you time to improve areas of your business that will increase its value and result in a more profitable sale.

Why a Practice Appraisal Is Essential

The appraisal document is the factual presentation used for many financial and legal issues. The appraisal defines what the practitioner has built: it is a statement of fact about a veterinarian's practice and what it is worth in today's market. It is not a report on practice management with suggestions for future growth or an alternative business plan. However, as will be discussed below, the appraisal has taken on new purposes and become a more important tool for professionals at different stages of their careers.

When created by professional appraisers (using their accreditations and standards, with absolutely no conflict of interest), the appraisal will assure a client of quality work and complete confidentiality. Their objectivity ensures that readers of the appraisal (accountants, lawyers, bankers, insurers and potential buyers) can be confident in it.

The appraisal can be used for many purposes: insurance, estate planning, borrowing of funds or refinancing of existing funds, buying another practice (sometimes they may be merged together) and sometimes for a family business transition from parent to child. Each of these scenarios requires the appraisal statement to document the value of the practice.

The ROI philosophy of the appraisal has always been that it is designed, written and formatted for the intended reader. The intended reader is a specific veterinarian. Lawyers and accountants, bankers, consultants and family members also read appraisals, but the intended reader is the veterinarian.

Thirty to forty years ago, the appraisal was not necessary because veterinary practices were perceived not to be worth very much. Why would practitioners pay $1,000 in 1972 to have their practice appraised if it was only going to sell for $5,000?

As the market has developed and the value of practices has risen substantially, the need for an appraisal has grown. These days, veterinary practices sell for widely divergent sums, depending on location, size, client list and many other factors, but it is safe to assume that the average sale price is higher than just a few years ago. Consequently, in today's changing economic environment, it is understandable that a banker, a lawyer, an accountant and a purchaser would want a proper appraisal.

Owners are sometimes reluctant to invest in the appraisal because they have a good idea of what their business is worth. Their accountant may have given them some advice. They've heard about other transactions and think, *That business is just like mine, so it is probably worth $500,000.* Today a buyer will not accept this type of reasoning. And you may be selling yourself short. Such assumptions are not very helpful. For example, you may have heard people say a practice should sell for at least one times gross. Using that logic, two offices that both bill $750,000 should sell for the same price of $750,000. But what if one has a net profit of 30 per cent and the other 50 per cent? Which would you buy? Hopefully, the one with the great net profit. The higher net profit business should be worth more! Gross is great, but net profit is always better!

When someone begins the process of selling their house, the first thing they do is interview two or three real estate agents. A part of that process, beyond interviewing them and asking about their marketing plan, is finding out what the agent believes the house is worth. In effect, they are getting two or three appraisals before they list the house.

Why would professionals, if they were thinking of transitioning their practice (the "baby" they have built from scratch over 30 or 40 years), not invest in a proper appraisal so that they know where they stand? The sale of your practice may represent one of the largest of your life. Why would you gamble?

Appraisals have become an absolutely essential planning tool. Today, it is mandatory for the sale of the business, at the very least. Appraisals are also becoming an elective product that veterinarians are pursuing in mid- or later career to explore the question "What are my options?" *If my business is worth half a million today, what will it be worth in 10 years? Will I be able to retire at age 57? Or 66? What should my retirement plan be?*

The Process

A good quality appraisal takes about a month for a professional firm to prepare from start to finish. It is necessary to identify, document and give value to the various goodwill factors involved in the practice as well as accurately record the details of all major practice assets: manufacturer, value, serial number, age, condition and colour.

An appraisal usually remains valid for about one to three years. This depends on major market fluctuations, which are unusual in veterinary medicine, or on if the practice goes through rapid changes such as expansion, new staff, new equipment or a change in location, ownership or leasing.

Experience dictates that the appraisal should not be free, even though some firms do offer it as part of their sale package. The fee normally charged is about $5,000 for the appraisal with a separate fee for the sale. Appraisal fees are 100 per cent tax deductible. A reputable professional appraisal will save the practitioner both time and money since it is far likelier to be accurate and to serve as a multi-use document. An experienced veterinary appraiser will also uncover additional value because of their specific knowledge of the industry and its nuances.

Essentially, the appraisal fee and the sale fee can be likened to how a veterinarian runs their business. A client who brings a patient to a veterinarian to have a medical procedure done does not expect a free treatment. So why would you expect to not pay for a quality service?

The Appraisal Generation Gap

Experience and observation reveal that there are at least two major groups of veterinarians. One is older (70-plus years old) and might be referred to as the traditional generation of veterinarians (the "old guard," if you will). Then there is a younger group, mostly encompassing the baby boomer generation. The boomers are the planners and consumers of professional services. They hire investment advisors, appraisers, brokers, accountants and consultants.

That senior generation is a more do-it-yourself (DIY) generation. Their thinking has been forged by a post–Depression era belief in frugal self-reliance. They often fix their own equipment. At home, they mow their own lawn, fix their own appliances and have many DIY projects on the go.

These veterinarians often do their own appraisals or happily use rules of thumb to their peril. Their appraisal is likely to be inaccurate and unacceptable to purchasers. Many will try to sell their own practice using a for sale by owner (FSBO) sign. This same practice occurs in housing real estate markets and reflects the same skepticism about the need for professional help and guidance.

As mentioned, the boomers (especially the younger cohort) are far more likely to hire a professional appraiser. They recognize that the appraisal has become a necessity. They are prudent and also recognize that they cannot leave their practice to their family to deal with after they die. Many locums who have served in a practice in which the practitioner has recently passed tell of the hardships the family faces in these cases where there are no professional appraisals or a suitable exit plan.

Martin Houser, a lawyer with Harris Sheaffer & Co. in Toronto, suggests that 50 per cent of Canadian business owners do not have a will. The appraisal *is* the will of the veterinarian's business. With an appraisal, veterinarians or their estate can sell the practice.

Seven Uses of a Professional Appraisal

Below are the top seven uses for an appraisal of a veterinarian's practice.

1. The appraisal should be reviewed with an accountant or other practice advisor to identify any opportunities for improvement or change.
2. An appraiser can meet with the veterinarian or their advisors in order to explain their methodology and

assist the veterinarian in preparing an exit plan.

3. The appraisal provides an opinion of the full replacement cost of the practice's leaseholds and equipment. The practitioner may wish to review their office contents insurance to be certain they are not under- or over-insured.

4. The negative adjustments in an appraisal are found on the calculation of the goodwill page. These are the "undesirable" aspects of the practice as purchasers see them. Some of these elements of goodwill can be changed to increase the value of the practice. Most at little or no cost.

5. A copy of the appraisal should be stored with the veterinarian's other valuable documents when uses 1–4 are complete. The veterinarian should attach a Letter of Direction, which can be prepared as part of the appraisal, to help in the event of their sudden death or disability. Call 1-888-764-4145 to obtain a copy of the ROI Letter of Direction.

6. Experienced appraisers can recommend companies and individuals that teach fundamental techniques to help veterinarians increase the practice's income.

7. Our years of service in the appraisal business has generated a national list of accountants, lawyers, bankers, insurance professionals and practice management consultants who can help with the next phase of veterinarian's career, whatever it may be.

In conclusion, hire a reputable professional to perform an appraisal of your practice at various stages of your career. Prepare a Letter of Direction and update it as necessary to help in your estate's proceedings in case of your untimely death.

CHAPTER 5

Late Career: Final Stages

• •

Hopefully you have enjoyed a profitable practice—many years of successfully looking after your clients to the best of your ability—and now you are ready to reap the rewards of your work by selling your practice and moving on to the next phase of your life.

Why Veterinarians Sell Their Practices

There are many questions wrapped around selling a practice, something veterinarians have spent their lives building. Often the decision is not a straightforward one. In working up to the sales decision, veterinarians often ask themselves and their advisors:

- Should I just be a clinician and not worry about running the business?

- Is now the best time to sell my practice?
- Do I sell the practice myself or use a professional to list and sell my practice?
- What is the value of my practice?
- A health situation is preventing me from working at my usual capacity. Is it time to sell?

As a company that advises veterinarians on buying, optimizing and selling practices so they can move into retirement, we've observed that the following three reasons are behind most sales.

1. Illness/Disability. The veterinarian has developed a serious health problem—perhaps a chronic illness or a disability that affects their ability to work, such as a hand injury. Many veterinarians will hang on in the hopes that they will get well and either work part-time or hire a temporary veterinarian while their health improves. This is understandable but usually a mistake. Approximately 75 per cent of veterinarians who go on major disability will not come back to work. If they keep their business in the interim, that business will suffer. Experience suggests it is wiser to sell the business and take the necessary steps and time to get well. If full health is restored, the veterinarian is free to start again with the benefit of hindsight.

2. Unrelenting fatigue. "That's enough management for me. I've done this for 30 years. I'm moving on. I'm tired." Sometimes it is after 40 years or even just 20 years, but for some veterinarians, there comes a time when they must move on. Many practitioners who are tired of full practice go into academia, consulting or

part-time veterinary medicine as a non-owner. This can be seen as part-time for life (PTFL) and freedom from ownership (FFO). Veterinarians who choose the route of PTFL and FFO can travel or work in different places. As a temporary locum veterinarian, they also can work for a month and then take a month off. There are many ways to stay in veterinary medicine without being committed to a five-days-a-week full-time practice and all the responsibilities that come with it.

However, the time may come that the fatigue is so deep and so pervasive that it becomes compassion fatigue. The trauma, illness, euthanasia and even abuse and neglect of animals can become so intense that the veterinarian finds it impossible to function. The syndrome creeps up; some of its classic symptoms include:

- Withdrawal from previously pleasurable activities and relationships,
- Sleeping and eating difficulties,
- Episodes of high anxiety,
- Physical ailments (e.g. chronic pain or gastrointestinal symptoms),
- Less tolerance for problems and others' stress,
- Feeling enormously drained by even small challenges,
- Loss of meaning and feelings of excitement about work,
- Feeling overwhelmed by the "residue" of emotional suffering, and
- Experiencing acute emotional pain (feeling neglected, misunderstood, sad, vulnerable and hopeless).

To complicate matters even further, as a veterinarian, you experience death five times more frequently than your counterparts in human medicine. If you ever find yourself in this situation, seek professional help. Take extended time off and, if necessary for your long-term well-being, sell the practice.

3. Financial freedom. Many veterinarians have achieved financial freedom because of their successful saving and investment plans. Some inherit wealth or have financially successful spouses who make retirement possible. These practitioners are the Freedom 55 or younger group who can move on from a veterinary career to do other things.

Finally, ensure you do these three crucial things before selling your practice:

1. Assemble your advisory team to guide you through the process—a lawyer, a banker, an accountant and a broker.
2. If you are truly retiring, detach yourself from the business—don't let the sales process become personal.
3. Sell when the time is right for you—when you are ready to move on to the next chapter in your life.

Preparing for the Sale of Your Practice

Start with an Exit Strategy

An exit strategy begins with calculating the amount of money necessary to meet your needs during retirement, then designing a plan to attain the goal. Financial planning can determine how much you need but may not show you how to amass it. At this point, increasing cash flow is crucial—a solid exit strategy will accomplish this.

Ideally, one should put an exit strategy in place at least four to five years prior to retirement. If you haven't and your retirement is imminent, consider developing a plan immediately. An exit strategy consists of the following steps:

1. Increase your cash flow to meet the current financial needs of your family. When you become free of immediate financial worries, you can increase cash flow to fully fund your pension.
2. Calculate how much money you will need during retirement to comfortably meet your personal and familial needs. Determine which pension plans and investments are suitable to achieve your financial goals.
3. Identify your successor and enter into appropriate legal contracts.

How to Increase Cash Flow and Practice Value

Three factors determine the marketability of a practice: how many people can step in and take over for you, its location and its cash flow. Carefully consider the following and remember to start these initiatives several years before you want to sell your practice.

- Institute a practice appraisal. You won't be able to move forward accurately and effectively if you don't have a benchmark. An appraisal will set a baseline for your practice value and help you set a future goal. It may also uncover some areas that need improvement.
- Look at the possibility of expanding or remodelling. Expanding can be costly, but a lot can be achieved with a basic physical reorganization of the clinic's space and a fresh coat of paint. Ask your staff for suggestions.
- Consider adding new or updated equipment or software. Ensure, however, that your choice(s) will add profitability and thus value to the practice. Before you buy, consider the needs of an incoming buyer: would they value the equipment or software as much as you do?
- Monitor your online reputation and take any needed action. Online reviews can make or break a sale.
- Every clinic needs an emergency service, a critical factor for buyers. If one is not available reasonably close to you, talk to other veterinarians in your area and either set one up or organize a call rotation schedule.
- Ensure there are no environmental or zoning concerns with your real estate.
- A clinic is only as good as its staff. A well-trained staff is your point of difference, especially in an urban practice with lots of competitors in the marketplace. Not only will a good staff make

money but a knowledgeable, compassionate and loyal staff can be a huge selling point to a potential buyer.

- It goes without saying that expense management and tracking is mandatory for a successful practice; ensure your accountant provides you with regular statements that track all your expenses. Ensure your books are clean and comprehensive. At a minimum, buyers want to see three years of training financials. Clean books show there are no skeletons lurking in any closets!
- Fees can be a sticky issue with clients, but you need to maintain reasonable fees to ensure the profitability of the practice. Do not put a new owner in the position of having to raise fees to maintain cash flow; institute timely fee increases.

Paying for Potential

Every veterinarian who is considering selling a practice should keep in mind that not only are you selling it as is, but you are also selling its *potential*. What does this potential look like?

- A room on the premises that could one day be converted into another exam room, which would allow the practice's production to grow beyond its current limitations, without having to move.
- Opportunities for prominent signage that have not been utilized.
- Simply re-marketing the practice.

- Improved follow-ups for continuing care and regular check-ups.
- Demographics in the area that have not been catered to by the practice thus far could be incorporated for future growth.

It takes a trained eye to spot unrealized practice potential—another reason to work with a skilled broker when the time comes to sell the practice.

Closing the Loop

In addition to the practice readiness tasks already mentioned, ensure the following have been attended to:

1. Secure your premises. If you do not own the building that houses your practice, review the lease for clauses related to demolition, sale of property or tenant relocation that could disrupt your business. Ensure the lease is transferable and has a sufficient term to allow a buyer to meet any lenders' requirements.
2. Ensure all employees, including associates, have written contracts. This step will help mitigate the purchaser's risk in the event of a future termination and make the practice more valuable.

Financial Requirements

Next, work with your advisory team—financial advisor, accountant and lawyer—to determine your financial needs until the end of your life. Discuss and decide how you will financially help your family—children, grandchildren, parents—and what you need to set aside for the unexpected. How much will you and your family need to enjoy the lifestyle you wish to maintain in retirement? Have a written financial/retirement plan, which addresses your income requirements, and update it regularly.

Succession Planning

You need to look after your clients. If you are a solo practitioner, what do you do? Wind down your practice? Take in a younger partner? Merge or sell the practice? Succession planning is a process that takes time; it should begin approximately five years before retirement so you can exit the practice at a time that suits you while maintaining maximum practice value.

Identify a Successor

Selling your practice is a life-changing event. The more work you do upfront with the appropriate professional advisors, the more you will benefit. Understand the factors that influence practice desirability, and once again, start the planning process well in advance!

Protecting the Value of the Business

Goodwill is of critical importance when buying or selling a practice; therefore the trading name of the practice is often a key asset and included in the sale. Regardless of the type of sale, a non-compete clause will invariably come up. The buyer wants assurance that the seller will not solicit staff or clients for a certain period of time. If the seller is retiring, this should not be a concern.

A Successful Sale

Let's summarize the six common factors that determine if the sale of a veterinary practice will succeed.

1. *Tax issues.* You have ensured that all back taxes are paid, reassuring any potential purchaser that they will not be inheriting any tax liabilities.
2. *Excellent record keeping.* You have tracked and understood the business of veterinarian medicine, along with keeping detailed patient notes and files. Thus your practice can be properly presented, which can result in a higher sale price.
3. *Full disclosure of all pertinent information.* You have been honest about all facets of your practice and are ready to answer any and all questions about it.
4. *Addressed weaknesses.* Things do not always flow smoothly in a practice. Problems crop up, such as tracking patients using an effective recall system. By disclosing this weakness that you have not had time to correct, the buyer will see an opportunity to correct the problem and end up with happier clients and more revenue.
5. *Absence of litigation.* You have ensured that there are no lawsuits pending or any investigation of your practice by a regulatory board.

6. *You have maintained your energy.* Selling a practice can take up to a year; there is a lot of work to do both before and after an offer has been accepted. Knowing this, you have assembled the required professional team who can take on the responsibility of answering questions about the business and management side of the practice that will come from the buyer's own professional team. Requested information is supplied completely and promptly and the buyer remains reassured that this is the practice they want to purchase. Finally, you have looked after your own health—you have ensured you remain rested so your energy level is high throughout the selling and closing process. Finally, you are proud of what you have accomplished in your professional life and know you are passing on a lucrative, happy practice.

After the Sale

A broker's work does not end on closing day. As brokers, we remain available to help the seller wrap up loose ends with staff, help the new buyer transition into the practice and be generally available for questions that may arise in the next 30 days.

Leaving a Legacy

Your legacy is the state of the practice you leave behind for the buyer; it is also the many happy clients, healthy patients and grateful staff who have learned and thrived under your tutelage.

But your legacy need not stop here; perhaps you will decide to teach after leaving your full-time practice and pass on your years of knowledge and experience to future veterinarians. You may want to write a book about your career or work with an animal charity. Legacy means different things to different people, but a common desire is to do something for others.

How would you like to be remembered?

CHAPTER 6

Retirement—It's about More Than Money

· ·

In Canada today, retirement messages from industry and governments centre mainly on our financial needs. But retirement can end up being a third of your life, and it deserves great consideration from all possible angles, not only financial ones. People become so obsessed with the question "How much will I need?" that they neglect thinking about what is equally important at this stage of life, namely "How will I spend these final years (yes, up to 30!) productively and happily?"

Yes, retirement means change, which is not always easy to accept, especially when it means leaving something you love doing. However, the time will come when forces—either internal or external—push you to retirement. Obviously, it's better to actively make the choice to retire, rather than having the decision thrust upon you. The two key words here, of course, are *planning ahead*.

The Myths of Retirement

Very few people are honest enough to admit that they are unhappy or disappointed in their retirement. But it is bound to happen; people work towards it for years, all the while dreaming about what their life will be like in retirement. But unfortunately, things don't always work out the way we envision. Watch out for some common retirement myths.

1. *Beware the paradise syndrome.* Some people imagine that retirement will be perfect—no stress, worries, financial or health problems. But everyday hassles will still exist; if you were not satisfied with your pre-retirement life, there is no guarantee that retirement will somehow change this. Have you considered what makes you happy, and will retirement allow you to pursue this? Your career gave you a sense of purpose, and you will still need to have a sense of purpose in retirement.

2. *You can decide at what age you wish to retire.* Not necessarily. Some people are forced to retire due to health problems, family issues or ongoing work stress that becomes unbearable

3. *Retirement means a life of leisure and idleness.* For many, retirement is a time to regenerate and re-energize one's outlook. It can be a time to focus on new endeavours.

4. *Retirement is basically an economic event.* Nothing could be further from the truth. It is the last phase of our lives, a time when we realize we cannot take good health for granted. It is a major psychological turning point, possibly a time to start over.

Picture Yourself in Retirement

Look ahead and imagine yourself living a retired life. Here are some questions to help you picture yourself in retirement so you can see how ready (or not) you are to retire.

- At what age do you want to retire?
- Will you work part-time at something else?
- Will you move?
- Will you purchase a vacation home?
- Will you retire abroad?
- Do you want to travel?
- Will you develop new hobbies?
- Will you spend more time with family—children, grandchildren?
- Do you want an active social life?
- Do you plan on volunteering?

Let's assume you are now seriously thinking about retirement, and the timing seems right. Here are some final considerations to help move your planning forward.

1. *Your finances.* You have had the necessary conversations with your financial planner. You know

how much you need to maintain your lifestyle, and you have saved what you need. You have the required insurance, your Powers of Attorney and an updated will in place.

2. *Your bucket list.* You have been thinking for years now about the things you want to achieve with the time you have left. Before retiring, you should know the answer to three key questions: What do I want to do? Where do I want to do it? Who do I want to do it with? Knowing answers to those questions will help give you purpose and a plan for how to spend your time. However, don't let the bucket list highs become an addiction; keep in mind what really matters in life—building bonds with family and community.

3. *Your health.* If your health is good, take advantage of this as you plan for retirement. If your spouse does not enjoy such good health, you may want to leave the practice earlier than you planned so you have time to do things together.

4. *Your spouse.* Many couples wait until the last minute to discuss how each sees life in retirement, so when the time comes, there may be discord. One may want a very active, engaged retirement; the other may just want to move to Florida and relax. It is critical that you and your partner start talking about retirement dreams years before you hang up the stethoscope for the last time so you can reach an agreement on how you are going to spend these precious last years.

As you can see, deciding when to retire is a complex decision with many moving parts. Think holistically about all the areas of your life affected by retirement—family issues, health issues, lifestyle goals and legacy opportunities. By giving these retirement considerations the time and attention they deserve, you can help ensure that your retirement gets off on the right foot.

Transitioning from full-time work to full retirement or even part-time work can be challenging. Prepare yourself by reading books and blogs on the topic; even better, find a mentor, a veterinarian who has been retired for a few years, and spend time with them to learn about the experience. A mentor can help you find the life balance that will work for you.

I'm Retired . . . Now What?

Retirement means change. It is the final phase of life and can be approached in many different ways, depending on your personality, interests and especially your health.

So let's talk about health. Yes, it may be time to sit back and re-evaluate your dreams and goals. But it is not the time to ignore your health, whatever its state. It is critical that you look after your body in every way possible. Eat properly, visit your physician regularly, manage your weight and, above all, exercise. According to a 2014 Bank of Montreal study, the four keys to longevity are:

1. *A healthy mind.* Try to incorporate mental exercises and aerobic exercise into your daily routine. If you feel stressed, learn to meditate and/or practice mindfulness. What's good for the heart is good for the brain.
2. *A healthy body.* Get adequate amounts of sleep (seven to eight hours per night) and regular physical activity; drink eight glasses of water per day; eat lots of greens, fruits and whole grains; reduce unhealthy fats and sugar and watch your alcohol consumption. Stretch your body to maintain flexibility.
3. *A strong social network.* Most people under-estimate the importance of social well-being and its connection to good health. Create a bucket list and take up those hobbies, or develop a new career. Consider volunteering or other community involvement.
4. *Financial stability.* Yes, you have a financial plan in place to look after your daily living and lifestyle expenses, but in all probability, you do not have a plan for long-term care. Too few Canadians understand the costs associated with aging and the increasing need for support and care until it is too late. The largest expenses in old age are medical and health care. There are proactive measures you can take; take the time to do some long-term care planning.

Retirement is a time to explore what is important to you—your values and life goals. You have the luxury of finding balance between leisure, perhaps part-time work and the pursuit of self-knowledge.

Yes, money is important in retirement; it affords you protection and comfort, independence, the lifestyle you wish and the ability to help family. But in the end, retirement is the opportunity to live out the dreams you never had time to enjoy and to be thankful for the life and career you chose.

However you choose to spend your retirement, enjoy it; you have earned it!

We would be remiss if we did not at least address the sad possible situation of your death coming as a sudden event for your family. When a sudden death of a business owner does occur, there are some regrettable consequences. If there are no clear and documented instructions to manage the affairs of the business, its value may begin to decline. Staff, suppliers and clients often become concerned about payments, and this may create a domino effect leading to a downward spiral of the business's overall value.

To prevent that, consider an emergency plan (much like a Power of Attorney) for the continuing management and care of the finances of the business.

Some argue that the shareholders agreement dictates what to do if one or more shareholders are unable to attend to and/or manage the business. But what about the sole-owner business? Have you documented who will act as the interim president and/or chief financial officer in order for your business (the large part of your life's work) to continue to run in its normal fashion?

CHAPTER 7

Tim's Tips

• •

This chapter provides a quick summary of some of the main points found in Part 1 of this book, as well as lessons learned from veterinarians and health care practitioners in general.

1. An astounding number of veterinarians do *not* have an exit plan, a Letter of Direction or a will. Unfortunately, some veterinarians will die suddenly and well before their time. Get a will and prepare a strategy for your demise! Do not leave your family to deal with the sale of your practice in addition to mourning your death.

If you suffer from a serious health ailment, take time and action to address this development as it pertains to your business. If necessary, sell your practice. In my experience, it rarely pays to try to keep your practice going in a haphazard way or to expect your associate(s) to get you through the rough times. Should your health be completely restored and you so desire, start again with the benefit of hindsight.

2. If a short illness or disability occurs, hire a locum veterinarian to carry on your practice. Locums have become an ever sounder way to deal with short-term illness or patient overflow.

3. Be aware of compassion fatigue when determining your work hours and the stresses involved. Veterinarians often have to euthanize their patients and deal with grieving clients. If this is not handled properly and with the right frame of mind, there can be severe repercussions. The much-used adage of "seek a balance between work and play" applies here. Be aware of the burnout factor and accept the fact that you can only provide quality care when your own personal needs have been met.

4. When selling a practice, never reveal your plans to staff or clients until the sale has been completed unconditionally.

5. Today, most graduating veterinarians are looking for careers in small animal veterinary medicine in major Canadian cities. This trend has not altered despite the many incentives available to locate in smaller towns and rural and remote areas. Seriously consider locating in non-major urban centres, whether your preference is to practice as a small or large animal veterinarian or both.

6. To date, the most prevalent and successful form of veterinary practice is the single-owner veterinary practice. In recent years, there has been some movement towards a more corporate-oriented, clinic-type business model. It remains to be seen if this form of veterinary service will gain momentum in the marketplace.

7. Young veterinarians seeking a practice to purchase must be cautious and patient. Finding the practice right for you takes time. Often, the right practice will present itself to you. This practice's clinical procedures and overall operational structure will mirror your own veterinary medicine philosophy.

8. Most graduating veterinarians are not ready to buy an existing practice or establish a new practice of their own for at least three to five years. Most recent graduates find success as an associate veterinarian in that interval. Often this development leads to a student/mentor relationship between the associate and the owner veterinarian.

9. Veterinarians opening a new practice in a mall-like setting in a major city are likely to experience two years of expenses exceeding income. It is prudent to have sufficient financing in place to account for this initial negative cash flow.

10. The referrals you receive from your clients are crucial to your success. Word of mouth will bring many new clients to your practice. It pays to treat your clients and patients well.

11. Be careful about discounting your fees for services. Once this practice becomes common knowledge, it is difficult to charge what your services are truly worth.

12. Single-owner veterinarians have a number of questions to ask themselves when it comes to practice facility size. If you are large animal veterinarian and are on the road most of the time and treat patients on-site, then a smaller practice facility works because all you need is enough space to allow for a receptionist and room for veterinary materials, medicines and equipment.

Small animal veterinarians need a functional reception area where clients can wait with their animals if necessary. There must be enough rooms for treatment (depending on the number of veterinarians working on-site at the same time). There should be an operating centre or area with a table, surgical instruments and equipment as well as sterilization facilities.

If kennels are part of your veterinary service, then more questions arise. How many do you need? Who looks after the animals?

Many more questions must be taken into consideration. Some of these are:

- Are animals kept overnight?
- Where do I locate?
- Will I have room for an associate or associates, technicians and office personnel?
- What are my washroom facilities?
- Should there be a staff room?
- Is there a quiet area where I can take a client to discuss a treatment procedure for their pet/animal?
- Can I treat exotics?
- What procedures can I do on-site and what needs to be farmed out to other veterinarians?

13. As a small animal veterinarian, know your patients. What percentage are dogs, cats, birds and so on? Plan your practice facility, time allocation and staff accordingly.

14. As a large animal veterinarian you may be aligned with a corporate business model that treats specific farm animals, zoo animals or other large creatures such as those found in marine parks. There are usually a number of governing regulations and rules that must be followed, and research findings may change your practice procedures from time to time.

15. Veterinarians should consider their facilities (waiting room, examining room, kennels, etc.) from the point of view of their patients. See and feel what they do, and try to experience their stay at your clinic from their perspective. Doing this exercise may lead to a better design of your facilities to meet your clients' and patients' needs.

16. Veterinarians should work in their specialized fields and consider what they can or can't do and know when to farm out procedures to other veterinary specialists.

17. When buying a veterinary practice, one of the most important considerations is the existing patient list. This is the *business* part of the practice you are buying. What are the financials generated by the patients? Determine who the patients are in terms of types, gender, age, special needs and so on. Consult with an advisor or do the analysis of what you are buying yourself. By doing so, you will reduce the number of surprises experienced after you have purchased the practice.

18. All practitioners should be aware that the face of veterinary medicine has been changing for some time now as more and more women enter the profession. In addition, more foreign-trained veterinarians and technicians have become an integral part of the Canadian veterinary profession.

19. Your practice is a business and requires that you make decisions to ensure that it survives financially. Devote time and effort to the business side to be successful.

20. Veterinarians should take into account that it has been predicted that investment in practice ownership may extend to non-veterinarians because of possible future deregulation. Corporate-style veterinary chains will continue to emerge and become a significant part of the veterinary industry.

21. Refrain from office romances. Maintain a friendly but professional relationship with all employees.

22. Communicate with your staff. Praise them for work well done. Gently remind them when they are not meeting your expectations. Compensation should be based on industry standards, seniority and, most importantly, on quality of work.

23. All veterinarians should have a well-defined office policy manual. It should clearly outline expectations between veterinarian and staff as well as inter-staff expectations. From time to time, this manual should be revised and staff informed of any changes.

24. When considering the sale of your veterinary practice, it is essential that you employ the services of a veterinary practice sales firm. When it comes to selling a practice by themselves, veterinarians often underestimate the value and undersell. Sometimes, quite innocently, they withhold critical information about their practice in terms of both its strengths and weaknesses. Hire a professional!

25. Many veterinarians feel that they should have retired earlier. Know that there can be a meaningful and rewarding life after veterinary medicine and practice ownership.

PART 2

· ·

SELECTED PAGES FROM *PROFITABLE PRACTICE* MAGAZINE

. . . .

As the editor of *Profitable Practice*, I am delighted to introduce Part 2 of this book. After having done numerous interviews with practising veterinarians and other health care professionals at all stages of their careers, one thing has become evident: health care professionals have much in common and have much to learn from each other.

Veterinarians are extremely well-trained practitioners and caregivers. They have empathy for both their patients and clients. Many of the daily decisions they make are based on financial considerations (both for their clients and for their own practices) and these decisions are often difficult and gut-wrenching.

In addition, there are moral, ethical and philosophical questions to be dealt with. When is euthanasia the best way to proceed? How does the animal's rights come into play and exactly what are those rights? How much pro bono work is enough? How are distressed and injured wildlife to be treated? These are just a few of the questions that arise for veterinarians everywhere.

The answers to these questions can sometimes be found in discussing these problems with other veterinarians and, somewhat surprisingly, with other health care practitioners. Consulting with and mentoring others, and not just within one's own profession, results in new perspectives and possible solutions to the questions veterinarians have. When this collective wisdom becomes part of the veterinary learning process and is shared, as it is here, good outcomes can result.

The wisdom that follows comes from interviews with veterinarians, guest columnists and ROI personnel. These insights are from their real world experiences.

JAMES RUDDY

CHAPTER 8

Columns by
Timothy A. Brown

. . . .

The Missing Bicycle

We just sold a professional practice. I attended the retirement reception last night. Around 150 clients came out to meet their old doctor of many years and to meet the new owner. Their spouses, the staff and a few industry advisors were all there to witness the event. It was touching and made me contemplative.

During the function, I approached the staff and asked, "How is the new guy working out?" and they were all very supportive and excited about the opportunity to work with a young, vibrant and handsome fellow. Not that my client, Dr. Mark, was not respected and admired, but he was getting a little grey and ready to move on.

One comment that a staff member made that really resonated with me was that she misses the bicycle. I asked her to explain. She told me that each morning when she would arrive, Dr. Mark would invariably be there first, and his bicycle would be at the back of the building where the staff parked. He is a dedicated cyclist and even rode in the winter months, rarely missing a day due to bad weather. I asked her why she missed the bicycle and she teared up and said, "I miss *him*, and when his bicycle is not there each day, it reminds me."

She said once again that she really likes her new boss and that she is happy, but the story is a simple reminder that we form relationships with our staff and any departure is an emotional event for all persons involved.

North of Highway 401

The benefits of practising and/or owning in these areas are abundant, and the practitioners that we have met with are some of the happiest, most relaxed and healthiest people we know. They have thriving practices and are regarded as the pillars of their communities. We always talk a little bit of business while we are with them and we can make the following observations, which are common in every single one of these practices. First, they are all booked up many weeks in advance. Second, most of them take six to ten weeks holiday a year. Third, very few of them work many evenings or Saturdays.

Their lifestyles are outstanding. Most of them live modestly within the community, but the secret they all share is that they can enjoy tremendous luxury holidays and are also able to enjoy the beauty, opportunities and activities that nature offers where they live and work. We often say that we wish a few more practitioners would come up and see some of the wonderful practices for sale in northern Ontario (or rural British Columbia, Alberta, Manitoba, Saskatchewan, Quebec, Atlantic Canada . . . you get the picture). Even if you initially agreed to stay only for five years, you may just stay a lifetime. We have many stories to share of clients who bought a practice from ROI in a small town more than 20 years ago. These owners are, for the most part, vibrant, beautiful and successful— and we marvel at the fact that many of them never saw themselves in this type of location, let alone that they would stay for decades.

Once again, we strongly encourage all health care professionals in this country to look at the rural and remote areas of Canada where you are needed. You can be a part of a group that makes a difference in the community in which you live. You will enjoy financial success and, needless to say, the purchase prices of these practices, the real estate and the other costs of living are substantially lower than in the big cities.

Hire the Buyer: Yes or No?

One question that many veterinarian practice owners ask (usually at midcareer when they want to slow down a little) is "Should I hire an associate?" Many then ponder these additional questions: If I hire an associate, what effect will it have on the practice (pros and cons)? Will an associate impact the fair market value and/or the salability of my practice?

There are many ways to look at associates. Small animal veterinarians are fortunate in that their clients come to their offices, so the addition of veterinary personnel power is not dependent on geography—it depends on client/patient flow, client/patient preferences and, most importantly, the lifestyle choices of the owner.

Most business owners want to hire a young, ambitious veterinarian and to see them grow in their skills and career. After all, we all had to start somewhere, and most of us had a mentor to guide us through the early stages of our career—the years when we make the most mistakes! Our informal research of owners who have hired associates (and many have also fired a few!) reveals that the large majority only sees the potential benefits of the associate; not much consideration is given to the possible detriments.

Here are some pros and cons.

Pros of hiring an associate
- Relieves you of extra client/patient load, allowing for shorter days (leaving at 3 or 4 p.m.!) and for longer vacations or more time for hobbies and family.
- Allows the practice to offer extended hours or to open the schedule for the owner to perform more complex treatments that are normally referred out.
- Generates higher gross income for the practice

and some economies of scale can be realized with supplies, lab costs, wages, etc.
- Increases use of the existing facility, equipment and staff capabilities.
- Provides for clinical companionship and the sharing of ideas with regard to complicated cases.
- If the relationship is successful, the associate may be a future purchaser.

Cons of hiring an associate

As to the day-to-day operations:
- Additional management duties (direct supervision and liability).
- Cost of integration into practice (signs, printing, training, legal fees for preparation of agreement).
- Loss of income in the initial phase as most owners "give up" some clients to get the associate started.
- Extra patient management time (non-income hours) is required of you to introduce the new associate and encourage patients to see them.
- "High-touch" patients may demand your attention to address their concerns or complaints if there are any personality conflicts.
- Staff often have trouble adapting to new personnel, and sometimes they don't know whose instructions to follow (especially when the owner is away).

As to the value of a practice:
- Associates intimidate buyers due the fear of incompatibility, and price is often a very contentious issue due to the many what-ifs.

- Although associates usually increase total gross income, they rarely increase your net income. Our firm believes that most owners actually subsidize their associates. Even when all cylinders are firing, typical profits are about 5–7 per cent of the associate's gross. One may ponder, *All that extra work for the owner and so little profit?* When you factor in the integration costs, it can take one to two years to recover your investment. By then, the associate may resign. Our firm's surveys suggest that the average length that associates stay at the same practice is less than three years because they often want to be an owner just like you!
- Increased gross usually means increased practice value, but the associate's presence intimidates buyers and a buyer will offer a lower price in most cases. In the end, you may sell for the same price as you would without an associate.

Conclusion

The decision to hire an associate should be based primarily on client/patient load and schedule demands. Lifestyle also needs to be considered. If you are hiring your buyer, be prepared: it may work out or it may not—and in the alternative, it could be detrimental to your practice if the former associate remains in the service area.

Do You Really Need a Broker?

As a professional, you have learned to listen to your

clients' questions and provide careful answers designed to educate them about the benefits of preventive care for their pet/animal. As a broker, I have similar experiences and a similar set of answers about our services.

Why do I need my practice appraised?

Much like your clients who do not understand the benefits of regular preventive care, some veterinarians are unaware of the benefits of a practice appraisal. An appraisal serves as a tool that addresses many career and business needs:

- Retirement and estate planning
- Property and personal insurance reviews
- Refinancing
- Practice sale
- Incorporating and freezing capital gains
- Uncovering business system inefficiencies

Our company has worked with veterinarians who cannot understand why their colleagues fail to invest in a practice appraisal. The benefits of doing so are numerous.

Why should I employ a broker to sell my practice?

Much like the trend towards do-it-yourself (DIY) home renovations, many practitioners take on the task of selling their own practices. While DIY can be a cost-efficient measure, common sense states that we get what we pay for. Ask yourself these questions:

- Would you sell your own car?
- Would you sell your own home?
- Would you sell your own practice?

For the majority, the answer may be "I would like to DIY and save the fees, but what are the results?" The market has proven that those who sell their own practices rarely achieve more than the result of a third-party professional who specializes in the art of selling the asset. The National Association of Realtors (a U.S.-based group) has studied the for sale by owner (FSBO) results versus those of realtors and found that in a large majority of sales, a realtor not only achieved a higher sale price (before commissions) but they usually negotiated more favourable terms for the seller, such as preferred closing dates and fewer "inclusions" (appliances, etc.). When I listen to stories of veterinarians who elected to sell their own practices, the results are not what you may expect. While many say the deal "more or less went as I thought it would" they also admit they made some miscalculations and failed to achieve what they first had anticipated. One of the key errors of the DIY veterinarian is not properly assessing what they own and its appropriate market value. Even with the aid of a professional appraisal, many admit they "gave away" some assets during the negotiations in order to induce a buyer into the final deal. Brokers, on the other hand, are not in the business of giving anything away. Other DIY vets reveal they did not understand some of the intricate strategies for reducing taxes and limiting the costs of selling.

Other benefits from brokered sales include:

- Adjusted closing dates
- Notification obligations for staff terminations
- Any outs of equipment leases
- Payouts of landlord fees to assign a premise lease

In short, a broker will almost always yield a higher total sale price—simply because it's in their best interest to do so. A broker should also be familiar with the most current tax structure or cost-reduction strategies for a selling veterinarian. It's wise to consult with a professional to be advised of recent changes. Some accountants, who are so busy with the bigger picture of taxation rules, admit they do not always know the finer points of a practice sale or the allocations of sale price that may be favourable to their clients.

In the end, I suggest that the DIY veterinarian will net the same proceeds from a practice sale when using a broker as when selling on their own. I also submit that you can choose to pay a commission to the broker and let them manage the deal, or you can pay the commission, in effect, to the buyer as they negotiate a better price and/or terms.

Many buyers see a DIY veterinarian as being unso-phisticated, and their immediate belief is *I'm going to get a good deal from this veterinarian.* While this may not be true, the perception is that the DIY veterinarian is a rookie and the buyer will gain an advantage by means of a lower sale price. Is that how you wish to be seen?

CHAPTER 9

Selected Guest Columns

· ·

This chapter presents the viewpoints of guest and staff writers in *Profitable Practice* magazine. The following four columns have been selected because they touch on topics that have not been covered in the main content of this book and because they are insightful and informative.

Millennials, MPOs and the Veterinary Marketplace

In this column, David Rourke, a sales representative at ROI Corporation, Brokerage, reveals the shifting nature of pet ownership and how millennials as a group affect veterinary practices, especially in urban centres. Practice owners, young and old, would be wise to heed his advice when it comes to their practices' marketing strategies.

There is a battle between the generations going on today, and while each generation likes to think that they are part of some special phenomenon, the reality is that shifting demographics happen in our society and are a central part of its evolution. Today, we are dealing with the allegedly over-stimulated, unfocused millennial generation that is endlessly checking their Facebook feeds or constantly texting their friends with no care for proper grammar. Indeed, they have invented a language of their own. Why call someone when you can text them just a few letters, then get right back to tweeting?

Being at the leading edge of the millennial generation, I have the benefit of being able to be critical of both my own generation and those that precede me—kind of a judgemental grey area. Of course, the disdain that everybody's favourite generation, the baby boomers, have for millennials is really not much different than how their parents, the Greatest Generation, felt about them when boomers were growing out their hair and driving their Volkswagens to those wild and crazy rock concerts.

Generational differences present an ongoing challenge to businesses and force them to constantly adapt and respond to the demographic variations. As I look at the veterinarian industry today, I see an interesting development that many readers of this article are well aware of, and I'm sure they are wondering how to respond to—namely, the millennial pet owner (MPO). I know these people exist in great numbers because my Facebook feed is full of them. They post pictures of their pets, they tell stories about them, they ask for advice on how to care for them and they create their own social media accounts for them. Very importantly, they ask for recommendations on which veterinarian they should visit.

I am in my early 30s, and, while more and more baby pictures are coming up on my feed, they are still heavily outnumbered by the never-ending pet photos. Now that we know these owners exist, we have to ask the question: Why do we need to care about a group of 20-something pet owners? I would strongly suggest that anyone planning to open a veterinary clinic over the next 20 years should not only care about but also prepare for the needs of the MPO.

The first thing to understand is the motivation of the MPO. While a boomer's early life goals were typically to get married, buy a house, have kids and then buy a pet by their early 30s, millennials are working on a different timeline. As evidenced by many reports, they are doing this all five to ten years later in life. This results in a void in their lives that they are overwhelmingly choosing to fill with pet ownership before they reach any other life milestone. For these owners, their pet is not "the family pet"—it is in fact their family. As such, they are treating these pets as if they were their kids and are willing to spend significant dollars on both health care and non-essential services and products for their pets.

Next, we will look at the spending habits of the MPO. While they have been unfairly labelled as the "Entitled Generation," they do have a different perspective on what expenses would be classified as non-discretionary. They are willing to spend more on products and services that they feel provide better quality, improved health or contribute to sustainability. However, these purchasing decisions are rarely made impulsively.

At a time when an overwhelming amount of information is available at our fingertips, millennials are experts in researching all sources before opening their wallets. Lastly, we have to consider technology. I'm going to avoid the marketing aspect here and focus on how to interact with millennials. It is no secret that we love and live on our smartphones.

We generally view phone calls as a nuisance and only use paper calendars as a statement of individuality. Finding ways to shift your communications with this group to email and text will not only help you do more business with them but also make it much easier.

Here is why this is important to all practice owners. For the last 30 years, the focus has been on catering to the habits of the boomers. This still works today because they are still the largest cohort of people with the most amount of spending power. However, the shift is just around the corner, and once it happens, the speed at which things will change will accelerate. We have reached the point where every year more and more boomers are leaving the workforce while millennials are entering that same workplace and will continue to do so for the next 15 years. The gap will continue to grow and it is expected that within the next few years millennials will hold more spending power as a group than boomers. This is a powerful force, and how practice owners and all business owners react to it will impact their future success. On the bright side, we are a generation of hardworking, empathetic and socially conscious individuals when we put down our phones—we just take a few more years to grow up.

Saint Cecil

This column by Graham Ruddy, a regular contributor to and an editorial assistant for Profitable Practice, *outlines a number of issues of interest to veterinarians. First and foremost is the issue of animal rights and conservation, followed by the issues of trophy hunting and poaching and finally the impact of social media to bring about change. Most veterinarians see themselves as advocates and protectors of animal rights and are often activists against the unnecessary slaughter of animals and the destruction of their habitats. Many veterinarians work unselfishly to heal injured wildlife and care for abandoned and abused pets.*

The South African company Martin Nel is under fire after they revealed they were planning to raffle tickets to win a safari to take part in an organized lion hunt. For animal lovers and conservationists, this comes too soon after the global uproar over the shooting of Cecil the lion, who has become both a celebrity and a martyr for animals that fall victim to poaching and trophy hunting. The raffle, which was planned in 2015, would have been held on February 5 at a hunting event in Las Vegas. It was cancelled after groups and individuals were critical of the proposed prize. This reaction was fuelled by what happened less than a year prior. On July 1, 2015, a dentist named Walter Palmer paid $50,000 to track and kill a lion. It is alleged that Palmer used bait to lure Cecil off Hwange National Park boundaries to an area where he shot the animal. Palmer, after collecting his trophy, became a target himself as Cecil's tragic death became front-page news. The result was a greater awareness of and debate about the world of commercial hunting.

Proponents of big game hunting, especially for predators such as big cats, argue that this is a conservatory effort. Hunting lions controls their population density, as too many lions can be a potential problem when their habitat is declining and they reside close to human centres. Lions are often victims of livestock owners, who make a point of destroying animals that harm their flock. The raffle held by Martin Nel argued that the hunt was orchestrated by an individual in the conservatory hunting community and that they were proud to be working with the Bubye Valley Conservancy. It was stated later, after the cancellation of the intended event, that the Bubye Valley Conservancy was not affiliated with the organizations surrounding the raffle and that it would stand by its own conservation practices that involved hunting. The fight against trophy hunting runs parallel with the current fight on poaching and the ivory trade. This issue is receiving increasing interest as more information comes to light about the victories and defeats in animal rights and welfare. One victory that occurred months after the shooting of Cecil was the Australian government's stance on hunting trophies. Australia has banned the movement of "trophies"—specifically the body parts of lions—in or out of the country. Wildlife trade offences committed in the country now face severe punishments, including 10 years in prison or a fine up to $170,000.

Social media has done much to bring the issue of animal rights and welfare to the world stage. It has provided a voice for animals and the organizations and individuals that represent them. These emphatic voices, with the Internet as their main social instrument, are doing much to prevent many inhumane practices against animals. The cancellation of the Martin Nel raffle is a testament to the awareness that was raised after the death of Cecil, which has generated a more compassionate view of not only animals on conservation land but all wildlife.

Sources

"Australia bans hunting 'trophies' from lions entering or leaving the country" by Oliver Milman (*The Guardian*, March 13, 2015).
"Cecil the lion hunter Walter Palmer faces calls for prosecution" by Matthew Weaver and Mahita Gajahan (*The Guardian*, July 29, 2015).
"Zimbabwe: Lion hunt raffle cancelled following global outrage" by Lara Rebello (*International Business Times*, January 5, 2016).

The Value of Pets and the Changing Role of the Urban Veterinarian

This column by Karen Henderson, managing associate editor of Profitable Practice, *explains why so many people today have pets and how important they are to our well-being. Further, the column analyzes how the role of urban veterinarians in the relationships between pets and owners has changed.*

I can't help but feel wonderful when I see a newborn pet exploring the world for the first time—all innocence, big eyes and bounce. They bring a welcome respite from the frantic urban lives too many of us lead today, with little time to stop and smell the roses. Pets make us slow down, for all sorts of reasons. As we shall see, pets play many critical roles in our lives.

Pets Are Stress Relievers

Pets have been proven to help alleviate human disease. Petting reduces stress; rhythmic petting or grooming can be comforting to your pet and you. When you connect with your pet in this way, oxytocin, the hormone related to stress and anxiety relief, is released, helping to reduce blood pressure and lower cortisol levels.

Pets Are Four Legged Healers

As most pet owners will verify, their pets regularly reward them with the gift of unconditional love, which can be therapeutic in a number of ways. Studies by the British Psychological Society revealed that dogs were beneficial to the well being of their owners and "boosted their self-esteem as well as feelings of autonomy and competence."

Got Winter Blues? Adopt A Cat

It's estimated that 11 million North Americans suffer from seasonal affective disorder (SAD). Dr. June Nick-olas, an English psychologist who carried out a five-year study of this disorder, reported that those who had a "Whiskers" sitting on their lap had 60 per cent fewer headaches, were 21 per cent less likely to catch a cold or the flu and suffered less insomnia, impatience and tension.

As Canadian Dr. Gifford-Jones writes, "So if the snow is still falling, the sky dark and ominous and you're suffering from SAD, don't reach for Prozac. Buy a cat."

Pets Can Monitor Health Changes

Pets are very sensitive to their owners' behaviour, which can be helpful for those who suffer from diabetes. Some animals can sense plummeting blood sugar levels before their owners can. "When diabetics get low blood sugar, they get ketoacidosis, which changes the smell of their breath, and trained dogs can pick up on that scent change," explains Christopher Buckley, director of veterinary medicine at the Humane Society of West Michigan in Kalamazoo. "It's not an innate ability in every dog, but they can be trained to do that." There are several organizations that specifically train dogs to aid diabetics, including Lions Foundation of Canada Dog Guides

(DogGuides.com/diabetic.html) and Canadian Alert Dogs Inc. (CanadianAlertDogs.com).

Dogs have been able to sniff out a variety of cancer types, including skin cancer, breast cancer and bladder cancer. In studies, dogs have successfully been trained to detect the disease using samples from known cancer patients and people without cancer. Pets have been reported to obsess over moles on their owners' bodies, which have turned out to be malignant melanoma. In a 2006 study, five dogs were trained to detect cancer based on breath samples. Once trained, the dogs were able to detect breast cancer with 88 per cent accuracy and lung cancer with 99 per cent accuracy. They could do this across all four stages of the diseases.

Some dogs have a talent for sniffing out the signs that a migraine is on the way and can pick up a scent and warn that a narcolepsy attack is coming on.

Pets Help Relieve Pain

Petting an animal releases endorphins—the same hormones that give a runner's high—and they are powerful pain relievers. In a study of therapy dogs at Mount Sinai Beth Israel in New York City, researchers followed 42 people who were receiving six weeks of intense chemotherapy and radiation therapy for head and neck cancer. Before each treatment session, all of the participants visited with a trained therapy dog for about 15 minutes. At the end of the study, the researchers found that although the participants' physical well-being decreased during treatment, their emotional and social well-being increased.

Pets Rescue Us

Loneliness is our modern day epidemic—it's considered a bigger health risk than obesity or smoking. Humans crave and need companionship; when it is not available, pets can compensate for this emptiness. Pets are social magnets. Whenever I meet a pet and owner, I invariably stop to chat about the pet and in the process strengthen both my social connections and those of other pet owners.

Alzheimer's disease is another modern epidemic that is becoming a bigger threat every day and everywhere. It does not take any scientific studies to see how pets can enhance the well-being of those with dementia. Whenever I took my dog, Oreo, to visit my father in a long-term care facility, the eyes of the residents with dementia lit up—she triggered their ability to relive and recount happy childhood days when they too owned a dog. Oreo with her quiet gentleness was able to, however briefly, bring joy back into the lives of those who have forgotten.

The Impact of Dr. Google

As more and more of us live with pets and, as shown above, depend on them to enhance or even save our lives, the burden on urban veterinarians appears to be increasing. With the developments in human and veterinary medicine, owners' expectations are becoming ever higher—we assume our veterinarians can now cure almost any disease, solve behavioural problems and successfully orchestrate a program of long-term care, similar to that for humans.

According to one veterinarian with whom I spoke, many owners now come to the clinic already having diagnosed the problem—thanks to Dr. Google. These owners expect a quick solution and see no value in a thorough examination of the pet or a discussion about treatment options—essentially preventing the veterinarian from doing their job.

Another challenge for veterinarians is dealing with those people who should not become pet owners because they are too ill themselves to provide proper care or are financially unable to afford needed treatment.

The Impact of Client Emotional Distress on Veterinarians' Well-Being

Because we depend so heavily on our pets, the inevitable end of life experience can be too much for owners to bear. Great love for a pet will ultimately bring great sorrow when the pet dies; losing a pet can be harder than losing a relative or a friend. The grief can be unbearable, as can the guilt—did we do enough at the end of our pet's life? Was it really time to euthanize? We turn to veterinarians with unanswerable questions like, "What would you do in my situation?" Here is where the (unappreciated at times) experience and compassion of veterinarians become invaluable. When the veterinarian and our pet tell us it's time, we need to believe them and follow their lead. The word *euthanize* means "good death"; our pets deserve this gift that we are fortunate enough to be able to give.

We have the proof—both scientific and objective—that pets make us happier and they make us healthier. In *Pets on the Couch*, Dr. Nicholas Dodman, DVM and program director of the Animal Behaviour Department of Clinical Sciences at Tufts University, chronicles research and case studies about how humans and other animals share neurological, emotional and psychological similarities; no wonder then that even Florence Nightingale said, "A small pet is often an excellent companion for the sick or long chronic cases, especially."

Bottom line: Have you ever wondered why there are so many pet videos on YouTube? Quite simply, they make us feel better—most of us get a little psychological pick-me-up. Adorable animals own the web and own our hearts for so many reasons. They are irreplaceable.

Sources

"8 ways animals help maintain human health" by Molly Kellner (*The Odyssey Online*, July 5, 2016).

"6 medical conditions that dogs can sniff out" by Jaymi Heimbuch (MNN.com, June 28, 2016).

"Got winter blues? Buy a cat" by W. Gifford-Jones (docgiff.com, February 20, 2014).

"Why do pets make us feel better?" by Amber Bauer (Cancer.net, April 23, 2015).

If They Could Only Talk

In this column, Dick Moody, a regular contributor to Profitable Practice, *reminisces about an earlier time when animals and pets were looked on differently. It provides a humorous account of growing up in rural Saskatoon and ends with a stark commentary on human behaviour.*

Long before Alf Wight—better known by his pen name James Herriot—began to write stories about his wonderful experiences as a young country veterinarian, my mother had caringly taught us to love all creatures great and small. Sadly she passed away before Herriot's delightful books about his hectic and usually hilarious life in England's Yorkshire Dales were available for her to read. And she would have so very much enjoyed the television programs that were developed from these books and were to become the most beloved and enduring shows ever produced about animals and their owners.

In James Herriot's stories, veterinarians are ever present in the daily life of a small Yorkshire community. But as a boy growing up through the long years of the Great Depression and the following years of the Second World War, even though I spent all my summer holidays in a small farming village, I never encountered a veterinarian there or in Saskatoon, my hometown. If I had, I might have become one.

I think the Handsaws, an imaginary cat family, originated in the fertile mind of my Uncle George. However he was invented, my two brothers and I grew up with daily offerings of sage advice from Rupert of Handsaw. In a lispy voice that was supposed to be catlike, my mother would present us with a variety of proverbs mixed in with helpful advice such as "Rupe says, 'The early bird gets the worm'—so don't be late for school." These "Rupisms" were not often welcomed, but if we accused my mother of creating these annoying bon mots, she would innocently say, "That wasn't my suggestion, it was Rupe's!"

I know lists are boring but it may be enlightening to enumerate the various animals that my mother persuaded us to give shelter to over the years.

To begin with, in the 1920s, my mother and father raised St. Bernard dogs. Bruce was a docile giant that whimpered to be freed if he was tied to my mother's sewing machine with a bit of thread. His wife, Lady, petulantly trashed the house if she wasn't taken with the family for car rides. Because there wasn't room in the car for two huge dogs, Bruce stayed at home with their pups whose appetites emptied the pantry and my dad's pocketbook. My mother had a canary that wouldn't sing, two mute love birds (one of whom began to merrily chirp when the other one died). And I had my best pal Joe, a gentle Airedale terrier that moved with our family from Detroit to Saskatoon after my father passed away in an accident in 1931.

In Saskatoon, we could have opened our own zoo. Over time, we had pets that included a turtle named Leonard; a pigeon called Feathers that bullied George, our bad tempered cat; pop-eyed goldfish in an outdoor pond; a pair of chinchillas that were supposed to produce children and make us rich but didn't; three chattering and nasty baby owls that ate hamburger while briefly imprisoned in a screened piano box; a clever crow called Joe; various hamsters and chipmunks that were forever escaping from their cages and hiding in a spring-filled couch and dozens of nervous tropical fish that were constantly found floating belly-up in a big tank generously populated with snails that failed miserably in keeping a clean house.

I had thought to mention Hank, the hawk that my brother raised from infancy, and perhaps add a few words about his parrot and cockatiel (which he insisted could talk) and his pet owl Nasty—but that would make this story too long. When our son earned school credits by working in an endangered animal shelter, home to aged lions and tigers without teeth and pythons without muscles, we asked him to cut lawns instead and learn landscaping skills.

Our zookeeping days are over. A remaining pet, a cat named Terrible Ted that attacks shoes (with or without feet in them) is developing traits that could earn him an early home in an endangered cat shelter.

For some time, humans have known animals communicate with each other, but we don't know what they say. But from what animals know about our mistreatment of our shared home—planet Earth—it shouldn't surprise us to learn that when they do speak, birds, bees and beasts are telling each other that humans are the dumbest animals in our polluted universe! And if he were still with us to say so, Rupert of Handsaw would heartily agree.

CHAPTER 10

Interviews with Veterinarians

• •

Interview with Dr. Nigel Skinner, Owner of Kew Beach Veterinary Hospital, Toronto, and Tracy MacTaggart, Practice Manager

There are a number of issues best addressed with direct discussions with the professionals who deal with them on a daily basis. The issue of the high rates of suicide among veterinarians is best revealed in Profitable Practice's *interview with Dr. Nigel Skinner and his wife, Tracy MacTaggart, by Karen Henderson. Not only does this interview reveal a lot about suicide rates and veterinarians but it also sheds light on the impact of social media on veterinary practices and the effect of clients' testimonies and comments regarding their veterinarian and their veterinary staff.*

Dr. Skinner, thank you for taking the time to answer my questions concerning your article about the unique stresses—*including suicide—that veterinarians face. What compelled you now to write so frankly about this sensitive topic?*

Nigel Skinner: Three factors compelled me to write the article. First was the growing awareness of the importance of psychological well-being in the workplace in a variety of different professions. Second was my wife, Tracy, coming on board about a year ago as our practice manager; coming from the outside, she was able to point out some things that were emotionally challenging for my staff that I had quite simply lost sight of, since I have been practicing for over 15 years. Finally, there has been a lot of talk online and in veterinary-specific venues about the growing suicide rate among veterinarians, the highest rate in any health care profession in many countries.

In the U.S., data indicated that nearly one in 10 U.S. veterinarians might experience serious psychological distress, and more than one in six might have contemplated suicide since graduation. Do we have any similar statistics for Canada?

Skinner: As far as I am aware, there are no such statistics for Canada. Studies done in the U.K., the U.S. and Australia all found the same high rate of veterinary suicide. However, I don't see any reason why Canada would be any different in this regard, since there are so many similarities in veterinary medicine between Canada and the U.S.

You write in the article, "Lately, there has been a signifi-
cant amount of chatter in the veterinary profession about the
types and the consequences of some of the stresses that vets
and the employees in veterinary clinics face." Why do think
there is more chatter about this issue now?

Skinner: Well, the first is the growing media attention
regarding mental health in the workplace, as I mentioned. The second is the suicide of two very well-
known and respected veterinarians in the U.S., Dr.
Shirley Koshi and Dr. Sophia Yin, which shocked the
veterinary world.

You also write: "According to an article from the Canadian
Veterinary Medical Association, the rate of suicide among
veterinarians is double that of dentists, more than double
that of medical doctors and four times the rate of the general
population." I think we can all agree that dentistry can be
stressful and that medical doctors are under considerable stress
at this time in Canada, so why do you think veterinarians
are at such risk?

Skinner: What I have learned from research into the
issues is that there can be many factors at play. The
first is the type of individual who is attracted to veterinary medicine. Veterinarians tend to be high achieving,
competitive and possibly introverted—perhaps prone
to isolation and depression. When I look at myself and
talk to other veterinarians, I admit that we tend to be
professionals who do not take criticism well and who
can take things very personally—as a result, we do a lot

of self-examination. These are traits that can make us good at what we do but can also be detrimental to our mental well-being. Access to means and the knowledge about how to administer drugs to end life certainly come into play. This unfortunately leads to a higher suicide success rate, even though the number of attempted suicides is lower than in other professions.

Finally, modern medicine has definitely progressed—we can do some magical things that don't happen by magic—but we can't fix everything. When we fall short, the veterinarian can feel they have failed, and the pet owner can feel the same, that the veterinarian has failed them. That's a very tough thing to deal with. We just have to keep on trying to educate our clients about the cost of providing a high level of care for their pets. Anyone I know who runs a really high-quality practice has to work with very tight margins; it's a difficult business to be in. And that's what both veterinarians and owners have to remember—veterinary medicine is a business, and if the owners cannot make a reasonable profit, they go out of business.

Tracy MacTaggart: Added to all this is the fact that there is no other profession where people have to make literally life and death decisions based on money, and no other profession where there are so many "experts" on pets—owners, breeders, trainers—who think they know so much that they can claim that your veterinarian is charging you too much or not giving you the best advice.

How do the U.S., U.K. and Australia, for example, cope with this very serious issue?

Skinner: I am not sure I can answer the question very specifically; what I do know is that mental health in the workplace is coming up more and more at conferences. The American Animal Association (aaha.org), with which we are affiliated, has come up with a whole series of guidelines, tools and online resources promoting wellness and life/work balance. I think we are at the start of something that will and must continue to evolve.

Do you think social media plays a role in exacerbating situations in which an owner is unhappy with their veterinarian?

MacTaggart: There is no doubt that social media can play a critical role for any business, both in the best and the worst ways. Nowadays, anyone with any opinion, be it positive or negative, can express it online. Unfortunately, there are far more negative than positive comments on the services or products that people purchase. We receive a lot of positive comments online, but we have also received some really scathing reviews from people who you can sense are never happy with anything. This reality has a big impact on the younger veterinarians, whose lives can revolve around social media.

One veterinarian told me that she had delivered the same service for the same cost to two different clients. One wrote a review saying the veterinarian was great, and the other said the service was below expectation. No constructive criticism was offered, and the veterinarian could not get the poor review off her mind. She then started questioning herself about her capabilities. Constructive criticism can be helpful because you can hopefully figure out how to fix the problem. Sheer negativity is destructive.

Skinner: Social media is not going away, so perhaps what we need to do is look more closely at how we react to it. In our staff meetings, we talk about all the feedback that we get; personally, if we get a comment that is wantonly destructive or anonymous, I will never read it. On the other hand, if someone complains that they had a 3:00 p.m. appointment and did not get seen until 4:00 p.m., I am going to try to figure out why that happened and, if possible, improve what we do.

What part of your practice generates the most stress for you?

Skinner: From a practical standpoint, quite honestly, it's managing the fluctuation in our volume from a cash flow perspective. From an emotional standpoint, it's not euthanasia. Euthanasia is a scared privilege that we as a profession are really lucky to be charged with. But once again, I have to go back to the money issue. When the care I want to provide for a particular pet is beyond the financial means of the owner, I need to find a compromise. We do as much as we can to bridge the gap, but we're often left pulled between what we know is best and what can be paid for or what we can absorb in losses. It would be so much easier for everyone if we could provide the best care and then bill a third party—just like the human health care system.

How do you personally deal with clients who feel you are "ripping them off"?

Skinner: This is a complex issue for sure. Clients unfortunately have no frame of reference for the costs involved in caring for their pets, since owners, for example, don't have to pay for their own X-rays or blood tests. I feel it's imperative that we educate clients so they understand the value of the services we provide—whether it's work hours or the need for expensive equipment. Also the College allows for considerable variability in fees charged between practices. Another issue is the emotions that are involved; owners have a strong emotional bond with their pets, and no one wants to be in the situation where they have to make care decisions based on financial constraints. But we have to have these conversations, and they can be extremely difficult. Some clients do feel they are being ripped off, but even when you try to explain the value you are providing, sometimes you are left with just a bad, awkward situation.

You write, "At our clinic, we have initiated a zero tolerance policy when it comes to clients being verbally or emotionally abusive to staff. I will recommend to every vet I know that they do the same." Why did you have to do this? Did it result from a particular incident?

Skinner: This did not result from one particular incident; what really prompted the policy was Tracy's feedback that some incidents—maybe half a dozen a year—were really taking a toll on the staff. When a staff member is reduced to tears and has to go home because of an abusive client, it's not right; Tracy was adamant that this needed to be addressed, no matter how infrequently this situation occurred. You never have to leave your shift at the Gap in tears, ever! The policy does not mean that when a client becomes very upset, they are out the door. It comes into play when a client accuses us of being uncaring, yelling at us or stating that we are unprofessional and only working for the money. A crisis happens more so when it's one particular person in a family whose behaviour has become continually unacceptable. When this is the case, we don't fire the family but state that another family member must now bring the pet to the clinic. The decision to stay with us is then up to the family— we will accommodate their wishes as much as we can.

Nigel, how do you personally handle the stress you encounter every day?

Skinner: It's something I have really had to learn and work on over the years. For me, it's a mix of very separate outside interests and physical activity each week. A couple of times a week, I play hockey, I go to the gym, do yoga, snowboard and rock climb—things that require real focus.

Interview with Dr. Andrea S. Coombs, DVM, OVC 1978

This next interview features a veterinarian who has chosen not to buy her own practice, works with the homeless and their pets and does much to alleviate the immense problem of pet abandonment, overpopulation and abuse. She was surprised and humbled that Profitable Practice *wanted to interview her. Here is her story, as told to James Ruddy, which reveals how she derives so much satisfaction from her profession and from her family.*

What and who influenced you to become a veterinarian?

I was always fascinated with animals, and at 14, I got a job working weekends at Kipewa Kennels, a breeding, training and boarding facility owned by Bill and Kathy McClure just outside Ottawa. He was a well-respected trainer, competitor and field trial judge of Brittany spaniels and English setters. I learned about the dogs, their care, breeding and training and the business of running a kennel. He was also an avid naturalist, so I learned much about the natural world around me as well. I was hooked!

Later, I was fortunate to get a job after school with the local village veterinarian, Dr. Sidney Pickett. His practice consisted mainly of dogs and cats. A high school classmate's father, Dr. Ken Hartin, was the local large animal veterinarian and I took any available opportunity to go on practice rounds with him to see cows, sheep and swine. My "team" of mentors was very supportive of my desire to become a veterinarian, and they were all very generous with their time and knowledge. I would not have achieved my dream had it not been for their encouragement and faith in my ability.

What is your area of expertise or specialty?

I spent roughly the first 15 years of my 35-year career in small animal practice in the GTA. Following that, I became involved in working with Dr. Jackie Jenkins at Wildcare, a wildlife rehabilitation centre in Vaughan, Ontario. I provided veterinary care for native Ontario wildlife with the goal of returning these wonderful creatures, small mammals, birds and reptiles back to their homes in the wild. I continued with Wildlife at a few facilities for roughly two decades while continuing to do some small animal practice as well. About 10 years ago, I found myself working in two animal shelters and am now working in shelter medicine at the Toronto Humane Society. My current position is staff veterinarian in the spay/neuter services there. I also volunteer with an organization that provides free spay and neuter surgeries for local managed feral colonies.

Describe a typical day for you.

I arrive at 7:30 a.m., just as the animals are arriving for surgery. For the next hour and a half, the technicians and I give each animal a physical examination to be certain that they are suitable for the procedures scheduled. We only work on young, healthy animals, and if we have concerns about the health of a particular cat or dog, surgery is delayed until the owner has the animal examined by their veterinarian. Only when the problem is resolved to that veterinarian's satisfaction is the animal rebooked for surgery at our facility. We provide low-cost surgery only by working with high numbers, and therefore we want to provide the safest procedures possible. Our results have been exceptional. Surgery begins when the animals have all been examined and pre-medicated and continues until all animals have been attended to. Typically, the number ranges between 25 and 30 surgeries per day.

When surgery is finished, the inevitable paperwork and logging in to charts is done, and monitoring of the animals in recovery continues until all are safely recovered from anesthesia. Prior to discharge, I examine the animals again and answer clients' questions or deal with any concerns I may have.

What has surprised you the most in your veterinary career?

The biggest surprise, or perhaps shock is a better word, came on my entrance into the world of shelter medicine. I had worked in practice for many years and never set foot in a shelter for more than a few minutes, nor was shelter medicine ever discussed at school. It was an overwhelming experience at first. I had no idea of the scope of health conditions of the animals that entered the system or the incredible number of animals involved. So many pets (unlike my own cherished ones at home) that were unwanted, discarded and begging for attention in cages and kennels . . . all as a result of human irresponsibility.

The pet overpopulation problem in Canada, the United States and indeed the whole world is staggering. The number of animals euthanized is horrific. As a practicing veterinarian, I had heard about the problem, but it takes on a whole new meaning when you are confronted with the sheer numbers and the level of care necessary for these animals.

What gives you satisfaction both professionally and personally?

As a new grad, my ambition was to help animals in need and make a difference in their lives. I spent the first part of my career in practice, then in wildlife and now in a shelter. I cannot count the number of animals involved, domestic or wild, but it must be in the tens of thousands over my 35 years and counting. I feel that I have had an impact, a quiet one, but one that pleases me greatly.

Wildlife has always been a fascination for me. My early years were spent in the national parks in the Rockies where the wildlife was abundant and varied in species. Wildlife rehabilitation is often a challenge. Funding is always a concern as there is no government support.

It is also a challenge because the purpose is to return the animals, orphaned or injured, to the wild. To do this, they must be fit enough to survive, to care for themselves, to reproduce and to care for offspring. Some are too badly damaged to be released back into their habitat. The ones we are able to release make all of our struggles and losses incredibly worthwhile. There is something about the ability to fly that defies description. To shelter a wounded bird, in pain and terror, with no understanding of either its inability to fly nor your intentions to help, is quite a responsibility. To open your gloved hand and release that bundle of feathers, be it robin, gull or raptor, and watch them fly again is extremely rewarding.

I became involved in the development of one of the early high volume/low cost spay/neuter clinics in Canada after training with an organization called Humane Alliance in North Carolina. We learned surgical techniques to provide rapid, safe procedures for large numbers of animals. I was attracted to this program because it is the only viable *proactive* step I have come across that deals with the vast pet overpopulation problem. Animal shelters are necessary in reaction to a problem created by humans. Education is a huge part of what shelters do, but it is clearly not enough in itself.

Veterinarians say to me, "Are you not enabling poor pet ownership in providing these services to owners that really shouldn't have the pet they can't afford in the first place?" Yes, perhaps, *but* the issue is that they do have this animal *now* and something needs to be done to prevent them from creating more animals that need to be nurtured in shelters that are already overcrowded and have few resources. People think about pets with their hearts and not their heads. And unfortunately some of them will make bad choices regarding the acquisition of pets. These are the ones I am happy to help because it is the animal and society that are the ultimate beneficiaries.

Personal satisfaction does come from my career but—and it may sound old-fashioned to say—the greatest accomplishment in my life would have to be my children. I have three adult children, all raised, educated and well into their careers and lives. They are all well liked by their peers and co-workers and are loved by all those important to my husband and myself. There can be no greater accomplishment than this in my opinion, and I am proud to have been their mother and to have watched them grow and take their place in society. Perhaps one of them could have wanted to follow in their mother's footsteps—but it wasn't in the cards. They all followed their own paths!

What would you change (if anything) about the nature, focus and perception of veterinary medicine as it presently exists in Canada today?

Students in every veterinary school should be required to observe the animal sheltering of all domestic species, large and small. As mentioned, I had no concept of the issues involved or the numbers affected until I was actually volunteering or working in a shelter. You need to see it to understand.

What do you do to unwind?

Spend time with family and pets (currently four dogs, three cats, two turtles). I like photography and I volunteer at a breakfast program at a local elementary school. I sing in the church choir, enjoy bird watching and riding (or should I say *falling off*) horses.

What advice would you give to the graduating veterinarian class of this year?

Same advice given to me: set aside some time to read/research on a regular basis. It's easier to do now because the ever-expanding volume of information is available online and can be accessed quickly. There are computers in our shelter and in almost all veterinary clinics that provide vets with data and advice to use in our practices and procedures that are available with the click of a mouse.

Lastly, I would advise them to spend as much time as they can with their family. Because children (if they have them) grow up in a heartbeat . . . try to be there as much as possible.

Interview with Dr. Darryl Bonder, Founder, Toronto Equine Hospital

Dr. Darryl Bonder presents an excellent example of a large animal veterinarian. He is an expert in equine veterinary medicine and highly regarded because of his extensive use of the latest technologies in his field and his belief in giving back to the community he serves. This interview by Karen Henderson touches on balance between the love of work and the love of family, as well as the role played by technology in veterinary medicine.

Thanks for taking time to speak with us. What made you choose equine veterinary medicine?

I have been a horse lover since I was a young child. This specialty just leapt out at me because it allowed me to combine my love of horses with biological science. I have been in this business 40 years.

I understand you used to teach.

Yes, I did occasional specialty lectures at [University of Guelph's Ontario Veterinary College] but did a lot of teaching at Humber College in the equine studies program. The program was discontinued; I think because it was a fairly expensive program to maintain—so they tore down the buildings and put up a parking lot.

How did the Toronto Equine Hospital come to be?

When my partner at the time and I had to vacate Humber College where we had our surgery, we looked for something close to Woodbine Racetrack. We found this building, which we gutted and set up as an equine hospital. It's literally one minute from the track.

How many equine hospitals are there in Canada?

I can speak better to Ontario; right now there are two private hospitals—Milton Equine and Toronto Equine. Of course, there is the university as well.

Do you have a typical day?

I could describe a typical day but there is really no such thing, as there is always the unknown. Today, I had an emergency at the track I had to deal with and so upset the schedule.

I get up at 4:30 every morning six days a week and I'm on the grounds of Woodbine by 6:00 a.m. I make my morning rounds of the barns I look after and talk to the trainers to learn about any issues the horses are facing regarding upcoming races. I plan my day so that between 8 and 8:30 a.m., I arrive at the hospital and start to delegate injections, etc., to the technicians. I will do the diagnostics, such as X-ray, ultrasound and endoscopy, but the technicians are highly trained— they are like nurses in human medicine—so we try to delegate as much as we can to them. I also diagnose lame horses by blocking them out; this means that we use local anesthesia to determine where a horse is experiencing pain. For example, if a horse is lame in the right forelimb where nothing is evident, if I anesthetize the foot, and the horse goes from lame to sound, I know the pain is originating in the foot. If the foot is fine, we'll start a blocking process and work our way up with regional blocks until I hit the spot where the horse goes sound. At that point, I may bring in X-ray or ultrasound. Here at the hospital in the afternoons, I may do surgeries or in-clinic scans; our nuclear medicine is extremely popular—we do the largest number of horses in this country when it comes to nuclear medicine or scintigraphy.

This diagnostic modality is one of the most sensitive tools available for evaluating the musculoskeletal system of the horse, allowing us to evaluate both soft tissue and bony structures. It's been a godsend to us.

How great is the physical risk to you and your staff when you work with these very large animals?

The risk is very real. We recently had a long-time staff member walk behind a horse, exercising all due precaution. Even though the horse was heavily sedated, it basically turned itself inside out, kicked her and blew her knee apart. So you have to always respect them, have almost a sixth sense or intuition about them. Fortunately, incidents like these are rare; I can usually tell what a horse is going to do before they do it—but not always! I was once asked to come into a stall to examine a horse that had a retained testicle. I had not even touched the horse, I had just bent down to look at the testicles when the horse went straight up into the air and came down on my head and my shoulders. Luckily, he just scuffed the side of my face and skull; if he had landed squarely on my skull, my brains would have been splattered all over the stall. When you are dealing with very smart, very quick, 1,200-pound creatures, things can happen.

The canine world is exploding with new services for various parts of the dog; do you offer a complete range of equine services here, all the way to dentistry for example?

The trend in both human and veterinary medicine is towards greater specialization; the explosion of knowledge makes it very difficult to be the James Herriot type of "do it all" practitioner. Within our practice, we do offer all services but tailored to individual practitioners. We have people who are surgically oriented, diagnostically oriented and those who are more dental or alternative therapy oriented.

How do you handle emergencies?

We have veterinarians on-call 24/7. Whenever there are races at Woodbine, a veterinarian will be present.

What are the most common problems in the horses that you see?

Basically we practice sports medicine, so we see a lot of lameness, orthopedic issues, bone lesions and soft tissue injuries. But we also deal with the animal on a more holistic basis when it comes to such things as respiratory infections or colic/abdominal pain. We take the horse's vital signs and evaluate how the horse is doing systemically by doing a rectal examination to see if there is a mass or twist in the gut. Because horses are unable to vomit like a dog or human can, we may insert a gastric tube to relieve pressure on the stomach.

Tell us about your new mobile service.

It is difficult for some people to get to the hospital if they are in more remote areas; also if their farm veterinarian lacks sports medicine expertise, we do use a farm in the Uxbridge area where we can meet up with people if they will trailer that far. But for the most part, we are here.

You spend most of your time with racehorses; will you accept any horse in your hospital, say a family pet?

Sure.

What's the most challenging situation you have ever encountered in this business?

The most difficult thing has been to maintain a work/life balance. I have four children and am soon to have eight grandchildren. I am fortunate in that my wife has always been very independent and can cope with the extremely long hours I work. When an emergency comes, we have to go.

The second challenge revolves around working with people. Aspiring students tell me they want to go into veterinary medicine because they love animals but not people. Well, this is the wrong profession for that attitude. We deal with people constantly, and if you're not a good, empathetic communicator, it will be the wrong profession for you.

The third challenge involves being a good business person; I don't care how good a veterinarian you are, if you're not a good business person you will not succeed in running a practice. Success means being able to motivate a staff so everyone pulls in the same direction, to be fiscally responsible and to present a service to clients that exceeds expectations at all times. The Internet has brought its own challenges, as any medical clinician will tell you.

Lastly, one of the most important challenges is just keeping up with the rapidity of change in the profession. If you are not malleable or able to respond quickly to the demands of your clients and to the advances in medicine, you are going to fall behind. I have always used the rule that if your practice is not changing at a rate that is faster than the general environment you are servicing, you will not succeed. In essence, being a pioneer at all times is so important.

How do you find the time to be a pioneer?

It's very difficult. We go to conferences of course, but I think a good imagination is critical, along with wanting to be at the forefront of the profession. We are so fortunate in our practice because we literally pioneered arthroscopic surgery for horses in this country. I was blessed to work under Dr. Robert Jackson who is known as the pioneer and father of arthroscopy in North America. He was the head of orthopedics at Toronto Western Hospital. He studied with Professor Watanabe in Japan at the University of Tokyo and literally brought arthroscopic technique to North America. The rest is history; it has become the most popular orthopedic technique going. We did the first equine surgery in 1978 or '79; I provided him with the information on the horse's knee joint, and he went in through a four-millimetre incision, pulled a loose piece of bone out of the joint and used one stitch to close it up. This procedure typically required a big incision, going in and looking for the piece and then sewing everything up. These types of procedures had terrific post-operative complications. This new approach was to me the future of equine orthopedics, without question. Dr. Jackson and I did many surgeries together, and his clinical fellows came out to my hospital to learn, as there were no textbooks, no papers, nothing. We were flying by the seat of our pants. Unfortunately, Dr. Jackson recently passed away, but his generosity and imagination were key to any success we have had at our hospital.

I know that you give back to the community—you donate time and materials to organizations. Can you expand on this?

I have always felt so lucky to be in a profession that I love and that has opened doors to me unimaginable in any other profession. I have done surgery, given talks and have made good friends all over the world. We know what huge challenges students face, and I think it's so important that we help ease their way by bringing them from virtually every corner of the

Earth to work with us; some have stayed in my family home for six months at a time and come into work with me every day. Also over the years we have done fundraisers for therapeutic riding organizations. The more you give, the more you receive, and that has certainly been the case with us.

If you had to do it all over, what would you do differently—or not?

I have been married for 40 years and in equine medicine for 40 years, and I wouldn't change a thing. I guess I would like to have had more time to spend with my family, but would I have achieved what I have without the support of the wife and kids I have? No way. There is always this conflict between work and family, and you can only spread yourself so thin. A lot of my work was not just for my personal, professional gratification, it was for my family—to be able to provide my children with the best education and home environment. At one point, I was president of an organization and sitting on various boards, so not only was I working all day, but I was also spending my evenings at meetings. My youngest son put it in perspective for me: he was about eight years old, and I had a student riding in the car with me on our way to an emergency. She asked my son what he wanted to be when he grew up. He had always said he wanted to be a veterinarian and work with horses like his dad, but on this occasion when asked the question, he said, "Oh no." When asked why, he replied (at eight years of age!), "I wouldn't have adequate time to spend with my children." That response put a dagger through my heart; at that point, I decided to serve out my remaining time on the boards and committees and then no more. It was one of the best things I ever did because I passed the torch to the younger generation. I also recently sold the practice to my colleagues and remain on as an employee.

What kind of opportunities do you see for students in equine veterinary medicine?

It's a rapidly changing climate, and I think the younger generation is getting it right as far as work/life balance goes. The pendulum swings back and forth to extremes; my generation was expected to work 80 to 90 hours a week, seven days a week. When I reduced it to six, some trainers got upset with me, saying they worked seven days, why could I not do the same? I responded that even God rested on the seventh day.

There are fewer horses around, which makes the field more competitive, and some of the industry is not on the most solid ground. The racing industry has gone through many changes in the past few years, resulting in a lot of unknown in the field. The sport horse world is still pretty solid, but it's neither easy nor inexpensive to own a horse. However, there is still opportunity. The best advice I could give a student is to get as much experience as you can, be open to different ideas and get yourself into the highest quality practice possible (not necessarily the highest paying practice) because mentorship is so important. Jump in with both feet, and don't expect to make oodles of money. My philosophy always was do good quality work, provide good service and the money will follow, whatever that is.

Finally, I know you are an avid cyclist; are you out for distance or speed?

I belong to a cycling club where I do both; the sport has been a passion of mine for decades. It's kept me fit, and as a stress release, it's probably saved my life. I average 200 to 250 kilometres a week during the season. In the winter, I do spin classes and have a bike on a trainer at home. I run with my dog, and no, I don't own a horse—my bike is my horse.

CHAPTER 11

Memorable Quotes from Selected Veterinarians

• •

Profitable Practice has interviewed many veterinarians on many issues. Here are some of the more noteworthy quotes packed with advice and common (and sometimes not-so-common) sense.

Dr. Barry MacEachern
You spend a lot of time treating wildlife. While this is very admirable, what are some of the pitfalls of treating wildlife that people may not know?

They can be dangerous! Dogs and cats can also be dangerous, but with wildlife they are very unpredictable. Extra precautions need to be taken for safety. Also there is the danger of disease transmission and therefore precautions need to be taken when handling cats or dogs in the same environment as wildlife. I find it difficult at times to find the information I need to help me with wildlife cases—there is not as much resource material about wildlife diseases. There is also more euthanasia in wildlife than I do with dog/cat patients. Any wild animal that cannot be fixed and returned to the wild is euthanized. Some days 50 per cent of the wildlife I look at are euthanized—this can really take its toll on one's spirit and staff morale.

Dr. Robert Lofsky

What do you tell a client whose pet is suffering and near the end?

That's tough. You have to empathize with them. Sometimes they just can't afford the procedures that might extend their pets' lives. As a vet, you have to know and accept the options and make these clear for them. You have to guide them and allow them to feel that you and they have done the best they can. A good indicator for them is to measure the number of good days their pet is having versus the not-so-good ones.

In the end, you and your client try to do what is best for the pet.

Dr. Elizabeth O'Brien

What is the best practice management advice you can give to young veterinarians starting out?

Forget the work/life balance that is so often promoted today. Young veterinarians should work long hours to build the foundation of their skills and eventually their practices. It is fun to experience all the types of procedures and to meet different people in the industry and learn from each experience. Later in their career is the time for a better balance between work and life.

Dr. Cheryl Yuill

What are your thoughts with regard to the state of veterinary practice and service in Canada today?

I return to the need for education of the general public, making them aware of the issues of neglect, overpopulation, proper nutrition and animal care and what is the makeup of a good pet or animal owner. There needs to be a unified veterinary voice educating, finding funding and volunteering time to help local, provincial and privately sponsored agencies to reduce animal abuse and improve overall animal care.

Dr. Christian Cumberbatch

As a new graduate, should you associate or go directly into solo practice?

Of course, it's an individual decision, but I suggest that graduates should associate first before making a decision about buying or starting a practice. For most, this is necessary in order to pay off debts and build sufficient capital to buy a practice. There is much to learn about the responsibilities of running a practice and the soft skills necessary—like bedside manner—that take time and observation to master. There are administrative and management decisions to be made daily with an eye to profit, payroll ratios, inventory controls and other considerations. These can be a turn-off to some people.

Dr. Chuck Lockton
What in your long and colourful veterinarian career gave you the most satisfaction?

Any live birth was always a thrill and still is, but particularly so if I had made a significant or perhaps crucial contribution—everything from foalings to the Caesarian birth of a nutria. Seeing the origin of new life is always an awesome privilege.

Dr. Angela Whelan
What advice would you give to recent graduates of veterinary medicine?

It is not just a love of animals that is going to keep you in this profession for a long time; you also have to have a compassion for life—the lives of the patients under your care, the lives of their owners, the lives of the people who you work with and the lives of your own family. Don't ever sacrifice one life for another; you will need all of them at one time or another. Remember too that it is not all about financial wealth; wealth comes in a variety of forms.

Dr. Vivian Jamieson
What are your main plans for retirement?

To live a more creative life—similar to most of the retired people I know. To travel—primarily off the beaten track and with a wildlife related focus. Retirement really is a rewarding phase of life—to have a successful career behind you and nothing to lose going forward. It's a time to learn new things and develop a new talent base.

CONCLUSION

. . . .

Owning a practice is a blessing and a privilege. Owner-ship is a temporary concept, as we all start as associates and most will end their career as an associate.

Being an owner is not for everyone. Human re-sources are the constant challenge of the owner and many professionals are horrible human resource man-gers. Becoming a veterinarian is a classic example of a profession where people want to *avoid* working with humans.

The owner who has a unique and specific skill set for human resources, amongst all the other clinical requirements, will find themselves in the top per cent of the profession, and the value of the practice will amply fund a retirement, often at an early age. The balance of professionals should examine their business skill set and carefully enter ownership knowing they will need help managing the business. Those who hire or contract out the management burden will be in the top 50 per cent of the profession. Their overheads may be higher than the top 20 per cent, but they will prosper and focus on their patients first. The remainder of professionals may be ideally suited for permanent, full- or part-time associateships, academia, research or working within the corporate model.

After a career of studying the key success factors of the top earning professionals, we have noticed that the number one indicator of success is charisma. People want leaders, and leaders with charisma are the most successful practice owners the authors have ever met.

ACKNOWLEDGEMENTS

· ·

We have many people to thank for their help in the writing and compiling of this book. First of all, to the thousands of Canadian veterinarians, many of whom we have had the pleasure to meet and converse with over the last few years. This book is in part a product of their stories, concerns and suggestions. They were unselfishly willing to share their observations in an effort to advance veterinary medicine to higher levels of proficiency and to help other veterinarians also seeking the answers that can be found in this book.

Second, we have to thank ROI's sales representatives, all of whom have dedicated many hours to helping our clients sell and buy veterinary practices. ROI personnel shared with us their insights and valuable observations about successful veterinary practices and procedures, which can be found in this book as well.

Much of this book draws from the wisdom found in the many articles about practice management in our *Profitable Practice* magazine. Some of these articles have been reprinted here for our readers. Thanks to James Ruddy, Karen Henderson and Graham Ruddy who manage to put out this informative and entertaining magazine. Thanks also to our friend and *Profitable Practice's* editorial consultant Dr. Milan Somborac. Thanks to Dan Pisek and Natalia Decius for helping to get the magazine off the ground. A special thanks to Linh Huynh and Ninh Hoang and their support staff at Advertising in Print for all they do for our magazine and for taking it to the next level.

I am indebted to my parents, Roy and Joan, for having the courage and fortitude to start the company so many years ago that has become ROI Corporation, Brokerage (ROI). My sisters Lanee, Debbie and Sally were also instrumental in ROI becoming a success. Special thanks to Lanee for organizing the process of the ROI Empirical Appraisal to a level I could only dream of. And to Debbie for encouraging me to write and publish. And to Sally for never-ending love and support. Finally, to Sandy Evans, my business partner, who was and remains instrumental in shaping and growing ROI to where it is today and who kept all the principals and personnel sane and focused in the process.

TIMOTHY A. BROWN

Veterinary Statistics and Pet Ownership Facts

Canadian Veterinary Statistics (2017)

Approximate number of practices in Canada: 3,240
Approximate number of veterinarians in Canada: 14,345

Female: 8,018
Male: 6,327
Provincially:
Alberta: 2,002
British Columbia: 1,693
Manitoba: 490
New Brunswick: 314
Newfoundland and Labrador: 115
Nova Scotia: 408
Prince Edward Island: 317
Ontario: 5,302
Quebec: 2,926

Saskatchewan: 746
Territories: 32
Pet Population:
Cats: 8.8 million
Dogs: 7.6 million

The statistics on veterinarians are from the Canadian Veterinary Medical Association database. The information is compiled by the CVMA based on data collected by provincial veterinary medical associations and the CVMA itself. See canadianveterinarians.net/about/statistics.

A 2016 survey of Canadians conducted by Kynetec on behalf of the Canadian Animal Health Institute is the source of the pet population information.

American Veterinary Statistics (2017)

PRIVATE CLINICAL PRACTICE	TOTAL AS OF DECEMBER 31, 2017	PERCENT OF TOTAL	MALE %	FEMALE %
Food animal exclusive	1,255	1.8%	77.6%	22.4%
Food animal predominant	3,223	4.5%	75.8%	24.2%
Mixed animal	4,220	5.9%	57.6%	42.4%
Companion animal predominant	6,368	8.9%	50.6%	49.4%
Companion animal exclusive	47,545	66.6%	37.0%	63.0%
Equine	4,043	5.7%	47.0%	53.0%

Other	293	0.4%	35.5%	64.5%
Species unspecified	4,446	6.2%	22.8%	77.2%
Total private practice	71,393	100%	41.6%	58.4%

PUBLIC & CORPORATE EMPLOYMENT	TOTAL AS OF DECEMBER 31, 2017	PERCENT OF TOTAL	MALE %	FEMALE %
College or university	6,878	40.9%	42.0%	58.0%
Federal government	1,858	11.0%	52.8%	47.2%
State or local government	1,109	6.6%	47.2%	52.8%
Uniformed services	761	4.5%	48.2%	51.6%
Industry	3,526	21.0%	54.1%	45.9%
Other public & corporate	2,689	16.0%	30.9%	69.1%
Total public & corporate	16,821	100%	44.3%	55.7%
Employment unknown	27,504			
Not listed above	2,017			
Total number of positions held by U.S. veterinarians	117,735			

Source:

"Market Research Statistics: U.S. Veterinarians 2017" by the American Veterinarian Medical Association (www.AVMA.org/KB/Resources/Statistics/Pages/Market-research-statistics-US-veterinarians.aspx).

Latest Canadian Pet Population Figures Released
Guelph, Ontario
January 23, 2017

The following information on pet population numbers for Canada are the result of a nation-wide survey conducted by Kynetec (formerly Ipsos) of over 2,006 pet-owning households and are consistent with historical tracking done by Kynetec on behalf of the Canadian Animal Health Institute (CAHI) since 2007.

Major Findings

- Cats outnumber dogs as household pets as of a 2016 survey. This was a continuation of a previous study in which cats again outnumbered dogs as pets.
- Pet ownership increased significantly from 2004 to 2016.
- Overall, approximately 41 per cent of Canadian households include at least one dog, and similarly around 37 per cent include at least one cat according to Colleen McElwain, CAHI Programs Director.
- Pet ownership, for those who choose it, has proven benefits for Canadians with regard to their health and social well-being.

For more information go to www.cahi-icsa.ca/

Press release
61 per cent of Canadians Own a Pet: GfK Survey
Toronto, ON, 24.05.2016

This GfK survey reveals much of the same information contained in the previous Kynetek Canada survey and adds information on pet ownership internationally. This online survey was conducted with over 27,000 consumers aged 15 or older in 22 countries. Fieldwork was completed in June 2015 and data are weighted to reflect the demographic composition of the online population age 15+ in each market. The countries included are Argentina, Australia, Belgium, Brazil, Canada, China, Czech Republic, France, Germany, Hong Kong, Italy, Japan, Mexico, Netherlands, Poland, Russia, South Korea, Spain, Sweden, Turkey, the U.K. and the U.S.

Major Highlights for Canada and the U.S.

- Canadians surpass the global average when it comes to pet ownership, with 61 per cent of the population owning a pet.
- Canadians prefer cats marginally over dogs when it comes to household pets.
- Canadian women and men are more likely to have a pet than their counterparts internationally.
- Americans outdo Canadians when it comes to pet ownership.
- 50 per cent of Americans own dogs while 39 per cent have a cat.
- American men compared to women are more likely to own a pet whereas in Canada the opposite is true.

Major Highlights Internationally

- Dogs are the most popular pets internationally, with Argentina leading the way.
- Cats are the second pet of choice internationally, with Russians owning the largest number.
- Women are more likely than men to own a dog or cat.
- More men than women own fish.

GfK is the trusted source of relevant market and consumer information that enables its clients to make smarter decisions.

For more information, go to www.gfk.com or follow @GfK on Twitter.